# Praxis and Physical Education Content Knowledge 5857 Study Guide 2024-2025

Mastering Praxis 5857 Exam with Comprehensive Study Material, Proven Strategies, Full-Length Practice Tests with Detailed Answer Explanations for Praxis Subject Assessments Exam

Test Treasure
PUBLICATION

# COPYRIGHT

All content, materials, and publications available on this website and through Test Treasure Publication's products, including but not limited to, study guides, flashcards, online materials, videos, graphics, logos, and text, are the property of Test Treasure Publication and are protected by United States and international copyright laws.

**Copyright © 2024-2025 Test Treasure Publication. All rights reserved.**

No part of these publications may be reproduced, distributed, or transmitted in any form or by any means, including photocopying, recording, or other electronic or mechanical methods, without the prior written permission of the publisher, except in the case of brief quotations embodied in critical reviews and certain other noncommercial uses permitted by copyright law.

**Permissions**

For permission requests, please write to the publisher, addressed "Attention: Permissions Coordinator," at the address below:

**Test Treasure Publication**

Email: support@testtreasure.com
Website: www.testtreasure.com

Unauthorized use or duplication of this material without express and written permission from this site's owner and/or author is strictly prohibited. Excerpts and links may be used, provided that full and clear credit is given to Test Treasure Publication with appropriate and specific direction to the original content.

## Trademarks

All trademarks, service marks, and trade names used within this website and Test Treasure Publication's products are proprietary to Test Treasure Publication or other respective owners that have granted Test Treasure Publication the right and license to use such intellectual property.

## Disclaimer

While every effort has been made to ensure the accuracy and completeness of the information contained in our products, Test Treasure Publication assumes no responsibility for errors, omissions, or contradictory interpretation of the subject matter herein. All information is provided "as is" without warranty of any kind.

## Governing Law

This website is controlled by Test Treasure Publication from our offices located in the state of California, USA. It can be accessed by most countries around the world. As each country has laws that may differ from those of California, by accessing our website, you agree that the statutes and laws of California, without regard to the conflict of laws and the United Nations Convention on the International Sales of Goods, will apply to all matters relating to the use of this website and the purchase of any products or services through this site.

# CONTENTS

| | |
|---|---|
| Introduction | 1 |
| Brief Overview of the Praxis HPE Content Knowledge Exam | 4 |
| Detailed Content Review | 8 |
| Study Schedules and Planning Advice | 11 |
| Frequently Asked Questions | 14 |
| 1. Physical Education Content Knowledge | 17 |
| 2. Student Growth and Development | 27 |
| 3. Management, Motivation, and Communication | 35 |
| 4. Planning, Instruction, and Student Assessment | 43 |
| 5. Collaboration, Reflection, and Technology | 50 |
| 6. Health Education as a Discipline | 58 |
| 7. Health Education Content | 65 |
| 8.1 Full-Length Practice Test 1 | 76 |
| 8.2 Answer Sheet - Practice Test 1 | 110 |
| 9.1 Full-Length Practice Test 2 | 122 |
| 9.2 Answer Sheet - Practice Test 2 | 156 |
| Test-Taking Strategies | 169 |
| Additional Resources | 172 |

Final Words                                         175

Explore Our Range of Study Guides                   177

# INTRODUCTION

Welcome to the comprehensive and invaluable resource that is the "Praxis Health and Physical Education Content Knowledge 5857 Study Guide 2024-2025." This book is your essential companion on the journey to becoming a certified health and physical education teacher, and it's brought to you by Test Treasure Publication, a dedicated educational partner committed to your success.

In the dynamic and ever-evolving field of education, we understand the importance of equipping future educators with the knowledge and tools they need to make a positive impact on the lives of students. The Praxis exam is a significant milestone on this path, and this study guide has been meticulously crafted to be your beacon of guidance and assurance.

**Unveiling Your Path to Success**

At Test Treasure Publication, we believe that exam preparation should be more than just a process; it should be an enlightening and fulfilling journey. We're here to not only help you pass the Praxis Health and Physical Education Content Knowledge 5857 exam but also to empower you with the knowledge, skills, and confidence to excel in your future teaching career.

This study guide is your key to unlocking the doors to the classroom, and it's designed to offer you a holistic and comprehensive understanding of the core principles and subjects relevant to health and physical education. Whether you're a prospective teacher, a career changer, or a dedicated educator looking to expand your horizons, this guide is your roadmap to success.

**What You'll Find Inside**

Our study guide is more than just a collection of facts and figures; it's a mentor, a companion, and a source of inspiration. Inside, you'll discover:

- A brief overview of the Praxis exam and its significance in your teaching journey.

- Detailed content reviews that delve into the core subjects of health and physical education.

- Study schedules and planning advice to help you make the most of your preparation time.

- Answers to frequently asked questions to address your concerns and provide clarity.

- Seven sections, each dedicated to a specific area of focus, ranging from physical education to health education.

- Test-taking strategies to optimize your performance on exam day.

- Additional resources, including recommended online materials and academic references.

- Final words of motivation to keep you inspired and focused.

- Not one, but two full-length practice tests, each with 100 questions and detailed answer explanations.

We believe in a personalized learning approach and a community-driven philosophy. Your aspirations are our aspirations, and we're committed to helping you transform your dreams into tangible achievements.

As you embark on this journey with Test Treasure Publication, you'll discover that your preparation extends beyond the classroom. We're preparing you not just for exams but for a future filled with boundless opportunities.

Join us on this extraordinary path to success, and let the light of knowledge guide your way. Your journey begins here.

# BRIEF OVERVIEW OF THE PRAXIS HPE CONTENT KNOWLEDGE EXAM

The "Praxis Health and Physical Education Content Knowledge 5857" exam is a crucial step for individuals seeking certification as health and physical education teachers. Administered by the Educational Testing Service (ETS), this exam evaluates candidates' knowledge and understanding of key concepts and principles essential for effective teaching in the field.

**Exam Pattern:**

- The exam consists of multiple-choice questions.

- The number of questions may vary, typically ranging from 120 to 150 questions.

- Candidates are provided with a designated amount of time to complete the exam, typically around 2 to 2.5 hours.

**Content Areas Covered:**

The exam covers a wide range of content areas relevant to health and physical education, including but not limited to:

- Basics of Physical Education

- Motor Learning and Skills

- Anatomy and Physiology in Physical Education
- Sports Psychology
- Fitness Assessment and Evaluation
- Childhood Development Theories
- Physical Development Milestones
- Cognitive Development in Children
- Social and Emotional Development
- Classroom Management Techniques
- Motivational Strategies
- Communication Skills for Teachers
- Conflict Resolution
- Curriculum Planning and Design
- Instructional Strategies
- Formative and Summative Assessments
- Feedback Mechanisms
- Teamwork and Collaboration in Education
- Reflective Teaching Practices
- Technology Integration in Physical Education

- Professional Development Resources
- Introduction to Health Education
- Health Promotion Theories
- Ethics in Health Education
- Community and Public Health
- Nutrition and Healthy Eating Habits
- Physical Activity and Wellness
- Mental and Emotional Health
- Substance Abuse Education
- Sexual Health Education

**Importance:**

- Passing the Praxis Health and Physical Education Content Knowledge exam is a requirement for individuals seeking certification as health and physical education teachers.
- Certification demonstrates that candidates possess the necessary knowledge and skills to effectively teach and promote health and physical activity among students.
- Certified teachers are better equipped to make a positive impact on the lives of their students, helping them lead healthier and more active lifestyles.
- The exam serves as a standard measure of competency in the field, en-

suring that certified teachers meet established criteria for excellence in health and physical education instruction.

In conclusion, the "Praxis Health and Physical Education Content Knowledge 5857" exam plays a crucial role in the certification process for aspiring health and physical education teachers. By assessing candidates' knowledge and understanding of key concepts, the exam helps ensure that certified teachers are well-prepared to educate and inspire future generations.

# DETAILED CONTENT REVIEW

Your journey to becoming a certified health and physical education teacher requires a solid understanding of the core principles and subjects integral to this field. The "Praxis Health and Physical Education Content Knowledge 5857 Study Guide 2024-2025" is your comprehensive resource for gaining the knowledge and skills you need to excel in this essential profession.

This detailed content review will provide you with an overview of the key subjects covered in this study guide. Each section is meticulously designed to empower you with the necessary knowledge to excel in the Praxis exam and, more importantly, in your future career as a teacher.

**Section 1: Physical Education Content Knowledge**
In this section, you will delve into the fundamentals of physical education, equipping yourself with the knowledge required to teach students about physical fitness, motor learning, anatomy, physiology, and sports psychology. This foundation will be instrumental in your ability to inspire and guide students towards healthier and more active lives.

**Section 2: Student Growth and Development**
Understanding the growth and development of students is paramount for any educator. This section explores childhood development theories, physical development milestones, cognitive development, and social and emotional development in children. You'll gain insights into how students learn and grow, allowing you to tailor your teaching to their unique needs.

**Section 3: Management, Motivation, and Communication**
Effective classroom management, motivation, and communication skills are essential for creating a positive and productive learning environment. Learn techniques for managing your classroom, strategies to motivate and engage your students, and effective communication skills that enable you to connect with your learners and address any conflicts that may arise.

**Section 4: Planning, Instruction, and Student Assessment**
Curriculum planning and design, instructional strategies, formative and summative assessments, and feedback mechanisms are the pillars of a successful teaching career. This section empowers you to design engaging lessons, assess student progress, and provide constructive feedback to foster their development.

**Section 5: Collaboration, Reflection, and Technology**
In today's educational landscape, collaboration and technology are critical components. Learn how to work effectively with colleagues, engage in reflective teaching practices, integrate technology into your physical education lessons, and discover professional development resources to stay current in your field.

**Section 6: Health Education as a Discipline**
Health education is a vital component of the curriculum. This section introduces you to the foundations of health education, health promotion theories, ethical considerations, and the role of community and public health in education. It equips you to educate students about the importance of healthy living.

**Section 7: Health Education Content**
Finally, delve into the specifics of health education content, covering topics such as nutrition and healthy eating habits, physical activity and wellness, mental and emotional health, substance abuse education, and sexual health education. You'll gain the knowledge to guide students in making informed and healthy choices.

**Your Path to Success**

This "Praxis Health and Physical Education Content Knowledge 5857 Study Guide" is not just a collection of facts and figures; it's your mentor, companion, and source of inspiration. It's designed to ensure that you not only pass the Praxis exam but also enter the classroom with the confidence to shape the lives of future generations.

As you journey through this content review, you'll discover that your preparation extends beyond the classroom. We're preparing you not just for exams but for a future filled with boundless opportunities.

Join us at Test Treasure Publication on this extraordinary path to success and let the light of knowledge guide your way.

# STUDY SCHEDULES AND PLANNING ADVICE

Preparing for the Praxis Health and Physical Education Content Knowledge 5857 exam is not just about studying; it's about planning, discipline, and making the most of your valuable time. This section of the study guide is dedicated to providing you with practical study schedules and planning advice to ensure that you prepare effectively and efficiently.

## Creating a Study Schedule:

1. **Assess Your Current Knowledge:** Before diving into your study schedule, take an initial practice test to identify your strengths and weaknesses. This will help you allocate more time to areas where you need improvement.

2. **Set Clear Goals:** Define your target score and break it down into smaller goals. Having clear objectives will keep you motivated throughout your preparation.

3. **Daily Study Sessions:** Dedicate a specific time each day for study sessions. Consistency is key, so choose a time that suits your daily routine.

4. **Weekly Targets:** Plan your study schedule on a weekly basis. Outline the topics and chapters you'll cover each week.

5. **Balance Subjects:** Distribute your study time evenly among the dif-

ferent sections and chapters. This ensures you have a well-rounded understanding of the material.

6. **Review and Practice:** Incorporate regular review sessions to reinforce your understanding of the material. Practice tests and quizzes are excellent tools for this.

## Effective Planning Advice:

1. **Use a Calendar:** Utilize a physical calendar or digital planning tools to schedule your study sessions and keep track of deadlines.

2. **Stay Organized:** Keep all your study materials, notes, and resources organized. An organized study space can enhance your focus.

3. **Take Breaks:** Don't underestimate the power of short breaks. Taking breaks between study sessions can help improve concentration.

4. **Seek Support:** If you encounter challenging topics, don't hesitate to seek help. Join study groups, consult teachers or professors, or use online resources for clarification.

5. **Stay Healthy:** A balanced diet, regular exercise, and adequate sleep are essential for maintaining your overall well-being and optimizing your cognitive abilities.

6. **Simulate Exam Conditions:** As you approach the exam date, practice under conditions similar to the actual exam. This includes taking full-length practice tests with a timer.

7. **Stay Positive:** Maintain a positive mindset throughout your preparation. Visualize your success and believe in your capabilities.

Remember, everyone's study needs are different, so tailor your schedule and planning to your specific requirements. Test Treasure Publication is here to guide you, but your dedication and commitment are the keys to your success. By following these study schedules and planning advice, you'll be better prepared to excel in the Praxis exam and embark on a rewarding career in health and physical education.

# FREQUENTLY ASKED QUESTIONS

As you embark on your journey to become a certified health and physical education teacher, you may have questions about the Praxis Health and Physical Education Content Knowledge 5857 exam and how to best prepare for it. This section is dedicated to answering some of the most common questions that students like you may have.

**1. What is the Praxis Health and Physical Education Content Knowledge 5857 exam?**

- The Praxis Health and Physical Education Content Knowledge 5857 exam is a standardized test designed to assess your knowledge and competency in health and physical education. It's a crucial step for individuals aspiring to become certified health and physical education teachers.

**2. How many questions are on the exam?**

- The number of questions on the exam may vary. It's essential to check the latest exam guidelines to know the exact number.

**3. What's the format of the exam?**

- The exam primarily consists of multiple-choice questions. The questions are designed to evaluate your understanding of the subjects related to health and physical education.

### 4. What's the time frame for the exam?

- Test-takers are allotted a specific time frame to complete the exam. The exact time limit can vary, so be sure to check the latest information provided by the administering body.

### 5. What score do I need to pass the Praxis exam?

- The passing score for the Praxis exam may vary, and it's usually determined by the state or institution where you're seeking certification. It's crucial to research and understand the passing score requirements in your specific region.

### 6. How can I best prepare for the exam?

- Effective preparation for the Praxis exam involves creating a study schedule, understanding the exam content, practicing with sample questions, and using quality study materials like this guide. It's also beneficial to take advantage of additional resources, such as online materials and academic references.

### 7. What's the role of Test Treasure Publication in my preparation?

- Test Treasure Publication is your trusted educational partner, committed to your success. We've designed this study guide to provide you with the knowledge, skills, and confidence you need to excel in the Praxis exam. Our resources act as mentors, instilling confidence, igniting passion, and guiding you toward your goals.

### 8. Can I find sample questions and practice tests in this guide?

- Absolutely! This study guide includes two full-length practice tests, each with 100 questions and detailed answer explanations. These practice tests are invaluable for simulating exam conditions and assessing your knowledge.

## 9. How can I make the most of my study time?

- To maximize your study time, create a clear study schedule, set achievable goals, stay organized, seek help when needed, and maintain a positive mindset. Regular practice, review, and simulation of exam conditions are also crucial.

## 10. What's the significance of passing the Praxis exam?

- Passing the Praxis exam is a significant achievement that demonstrates your readiness to educate and inspire students in the subjects of health and physical education. It opens doors to teaching opportunities in K-12 schools, where you can positively impact the lives of students.

We hope these answers provide clarity and guidance as you prepare for the Praxis Health and Physical Education Content Knowledge 5857 exam.

# 1

# PHYSICAL EDUCATION CONTENT KNOWLEDGE

## Basics of Physical Education

Alright, let's dive into the world of physical education and unravel its tangled roots. We're going way back to ancient Greece, where people worshipped physical fitness like it was the holy grail of education. Fast forward to today, and physical education is taught in schools all over the globe, adapting to fit the changing needs of society.

Now, physical education is a big deal. It shapes us from head to toe, inside and out. We owe a lot of that to the amazing physical education teachers who introduce us to a whole range of activities and sports. They help us flex our coordination, strength, flexibility, and endurance muscles. But it's not just about getting fit; it's about so much more. Through all those activities, we learn about teamwork, discipline, perseverance, and being a good sport.

But it's not just about running around and sweating. Physical education is a class that goes beyond the gym walls. It's a complete package deal. We learn about health and wellness, the science behind how our bodies work, what to eat, and the principles of exercise. This knowledge lets us take charge of our own well-being. It's like having a secret weapon to make informed choices about our health.

And being physically literate is a big deal too. It's not just something for the books or for the years we spend at school. It's about being equipped with the skills, knowledge, and confidence to stay active for life. We're talking about making a lifelong commitment to our health, which leads to better lives overall. It's all about thriving, folks.

Now, as the world of physical education keeps changing, we need to keep up. That's where this study guide comes in handy. It's gonna give you all the groundwork you need to crush the Praxis Health and Physical Education Content Knowledge exam. We'll cover everything from the olden days to the newest research out there. Together, we'll tackle the ins and outs of physical education, and give you the tools to thrive in both your studies and your career.

So buckle up, my friend, because we're about to take a wild ride through the world of physical education. This journey is gonna shine a light on all the amazing things within its realm. We're setting sail towards extraordinary success. Let's embrace the challenge and come out the other side as well-rounded individuals who are not just physically fit, but also intellectually, emotionally, and socially thriving.

## Motor Learning and Skills Development

First and foremost, let's start by getting to the heart of this thing. Motor learning, my friend, is all about how we acquire, improve, and perfect motor skills. It's like this intricate dance between what we see, what we know, and what we do, helping us become absolute pros at moving our bodies.

Within the realm of motor learning, we've got these two different types of skills: fine motor skills and gross motor skills. Fine motor skills are all about having the masterful touch, like being able to delicately handle objects or do fiddly tasks with our hands. Think of a surgeon delicately sewing up a wound or an artist using a teeny, tiny brush to make the most intricate strokes on a canvas. It's all about using those tiny muscles, having control, and being as smooth as butter.

But then we've got these gross motor skills, which are all about the big stuff. It's like a whole-body performance, ya know? Picture a gymnast doing flips and twists on a beam like it's no big deal or a basketball player dribbling and shooting like they were born with the ball in their hands. Gross motor skills involve all kinds of movement like running, jumping, kicking, throwing, and catching. They're what keep us moving in our everyday lives and make us shine on the sports field.

Now, let's go deep into this world of motor learning and skill-building. There are two major players that shape our journey to becoming masters: practice and feedback. Practice is the holy grail, my friend. The more we do something, the better we get at it. It's like going from being a newbie who can barely tie their shoelaces to a pro who can do it with their eyes closed. Practice makes us fluent and effortless with our movements.

But practice isn't the only thing we need. We also need that precious feedback. Feedback is like the North Star, showing us the way. It lets us know when we're doing something right and when we need to make improvements. It can come from someone telling us what to do, showing us how to do it, or even just feeling what's happening. Feedback is what helps us find that sweet spot of perfect movement.

And let me tell ya, having a good coach or teacher makes all the difference in the world. They know how to guide us on this journey. They give us clear instructions, show us how it's done, and break things down into manageable steps. With their support and belief in us, they help us overcome obstacles and keep going until we reach the top.

But here's the thing, my friend. Motor learning and skill-building aren't just about what we do with our bodies. It's a whole mind and heart thing too. When we engage in motor tasks, we're also learning all about what those tasks require, how they feel, and how to solve the problems that come up. And let's not forget the emotions that come with it all. Sometimes it's pure joy and satisfaction, and other times it's frustration and disappointment. Understanding our thoughts and feelings is key to getting the most out of this whole learning process.

So get ready, my friend, because we're about to dive deep into the theories, models, and practical applications of motor learning and skill-building. We'll explore things like how we go through different stages of learning, how we can transfer our skills to new situations, how our bodies control movement, and how different factors affect our ability to learn new skills. By the time we're done, you'll have a whole new appreciation for the wonder of human movement and the incredible potential we all have within us.

So buckle up, my friend. We're about to embark on an incredible journey into the world of motor learning and skill-building. And together, we're going to uncover the secrets to moving like a boss, performing at our best, and embracing physical activity for life.

## Anatomy and Physiology in Physical Education

Alright, hold up a sec. Let's take a step back and really dive into the world of Anatomy and Physiology in Physical Education. This stuff goes way back, back to ancient Egypt, where the OGs were already getting down and dirty, dissecting cadavers and checking out what makes us tick. They were like the first-ever body explorers, peeling back layers of the human puzzle.

Fast forward a few centuries, and the Renaissance period kicks in, shaking things up big time. We got Leonardo da Vinci and Andreas Vesalius on the scene, doing some serious dissection and sketches. They took this whole thing to a whole new level, breaking free from the old school thoughts about the human body and going all methodical and evidence-based on us.

Now let's zoom in a bit more to the present day. Medical tech and scientific research have hit the turbo button. X-rays, CT scans, MRI scans - they're like our secret little windows into the hidden depths of our bodies. We can now see all these intricate details that were once locked away. And whoa, hold on tight, genetics and molecular biology have busted open the secrets of our DNA. Talk about learning more about who we really are.

But what's the big deal with all this Anatomy and Physiology stuff when it comes to Physical Education? Well, it's like the backbone, the rock-solid foundation. Understanding our bodies gives us the keys to unlocking the secrets of movement, exercise, and health. It's like having the insider scoop on how muscles, bones, and joints all work together. We can see how it all ties into athletic performance and keeping injuries at bay. It's like the magic behind the curtain.

And it doesn't stop there. Physiology is like the next level of this body party. It's like peering into how our bodies function during exercise, how they adapt to training, and how they bounce back after giving it our all. It's like learning the secret sauce to maximizing our workouts and keeping our bodies in top shape.

But hey, don't just take my word for it. This knowledge isn't just for athletes or gym buffs. It's for everyone who cares about their health and wellbeing. Once you understand how your body is put together, you can make smarter choices. You can design workouts that suit your body's needs and goals. You can see how exercise actually impacts your body - the good and the not-so-good.

So let's embark on this journey, my friends. Let's take a moment to appreciate the mind-blowing wonder that is our own bodies. We're in this together, peeling back the layers and unlocking the mysteries of human anatomy. With this knowledge in our hands, we'll reach new heights in Physical Education and let our bodies shine bright.

## Sports Psychology in Physical Education

Introduction to Sports Psychology:

As I journey into the fascinating realm of sports psychology, I am blown away by just how much it can impact an athlete's performance. It's not just about being physically fit, but about tapping into the power of our minds to achieve incredible things. By understanding sports psychology, us physical education pros can unlock the hidden potential in our students and guide them towards achieving greatness.

Motivation and Goal Setting:

Motivation is what drives every outstanding athlete out there. In this section, we'll dig into different theories and techniques that can be used to inspire and energize our students. From theories like self-determination to strategies for setting goals, we'll explore how we can create an environment that sparks passion and keeps that fire burning.

Mental Toughness:

Let's talk about mental toughness, folks. It's what separates the winners from the rest of the pack. It's the ability to stay focused, resilient, and determined when life throws its curveballs. Mental toughness is a crucial ingredient for success both on the field and in physical education. So, buckle up as we dive into this concept and discover strategies for boosting resilience, managing stress, and embracing a positive mindset.

Visual Imagery and Mental Rehearsal:

Picture this: athletes using visualization to level up their game. They create these vivid mental images of themselves executing perfect techniques or achieving their wildest dreams. It's like they're creating a mind-map for success. We'll dive into the science behind visual imagery and also give you some practical exercises to incorporate this technique into your physical education training. Get ready to unleash the power of your imagination.

Attention and Concentration:

In this fast-paced world of sports and physical education, staying focused is crucial. It can be the difference between winning and losing, my friends. So, let's dig into some techniques for improving your attention span, concentration, and mindfulness. With these tools in your belt, you'll be able to tap into your full potential, no distractions holding you back.

Arousal and Anxiety Management:

Let's talk about finding that sweet spot, where you're amped up but not too much, and anxiety doesn't get the best of you. Arousal and anxiety play a big role in how well we perform in sports. Too much can lead to tension and a dip in performance, while too little leaves us feeling sluggish and uninspired. So, we'll explore strategies for managing your arousal levels, reducing anxiety, and finding that optimal state of mental readiness for peak performance.

Building Self-Confidence:

Confidence, my friends, is the foundation of success in sports. We're going to take a deep dive into what factors contribute to self-confidence and explore techniques for building and maintaining this essential attribute. When you have self-belief, there's no limit to what you can achieve. Get ready to break through those barriers and exceed your own expectations.

Team Dynamics and Leadership:

In sports, it's all about teamwork and effective leadership. We'll explore the nitty-gritty of team dynamics, taking a close look at how individuals contribute to the group effort. But wait, there's more! We'll also delve into the qualities and skills needed to be an effective leader, empowering you to guide and inspire your teammates towards collaborative excellence. Together, we'll become a force to be reckoned with.

Sports Psychology in Competition:

Now, let's take what we've learned about sports psychology and apply it to the big stage. From pre-game rituals to handling the pressure that comes with high-stakes matches, we'll dive into techniques for optimizing your performance in these intense situations. Armed with these mental strategies, you'll be able to embrace your competitive spirit and rise to the occasion when it counts.

As I wrap up this chapter on sports psychology in physical education, I am reminded once again of the incredible power of the mind in shaping our athletic performance. By incorporating these principles and techniques into our teaching practice, we can truly unleash the untapped potential within our students. So, join me on this journey where psychology and sports intertwine, and together, we'll ignite a new era of excellence in physical education.

## Fitness Assessment and Evaluation in Physical Education

Alright, let's dive into this fitness assessment process. The first step is all about getting the lowdown on the student's medical history, exercise habits, and anything else that could affect their fitness journey. It's like laying the foundation, making sure we've got all the deets to customize their evaluation based on their specific needs and limitations.

Once we've gathered all that important info, we can move on to the fun part - choosing the right assessments. We've got a whole range of tests to cover different aspects of fitness: cardio endurance, muscular strength, flexibility, body composition, and motor skills. We want to see the big picture, so we gotta hit 'em all.

To see how well the heart and lungs are pumping and oxygenating those muscles, we've got tests like the VO2 max and the good old 1.5-mile run/walk. The goal is to measure their aerobic fitness, how efficiently their body can use oxygen during exercise. On the flip side, we've got tests like push-ups, sit-ups, or even using a handgrip dynamometer to check out their muscular strength and endurance. We want to see if they can push through repetitive movements without tapping out.

Flexibility is also a biggie. We want to see how well they can move those joints and if their range of motion is on point. So, we bring in the sit-and-reach test, where they stretch their hammies and lower back to the max while sitting down.

Now, body composition. We want to know the proportion of fat, muscle, and bone in their body. We can go with methods like calculating BMI, skinfold measurements, or using bioelectrical impedance analysis. It's all about knowing what's going on inside and out.

And last but not least, we check out their motor skills. Can they run, jump, throw, and catch like a pro? These assessments give us the scoop on their coordination, balance, and agility. It's like a little peek into their movement abilities.

Once we've got all the data from these assessments, it's time to put on our lab coats and analyze it. We're comparing their results to the norms, trying to figure out where they're at and what areas need some extra love. This big picture view gives us a starting point and a roadmap for setting goals that are actually achievable.

But hey, this is more than just numbers and results. We gotta share this info with the students and their parents to get them on board too. We're all in this together, after all. So, we need to give them the full picture - what they're rocking at, what needs some work, and how we're gonna tackle it. It's all about creating that action plan and supporting them on their fitness journey.

In the end, fitness assessment and evaluation are like the secret sauce to optimal health and physical well-being. We're not just throwing random workouts at these students, we're tailoring their fitness plans, tracking their progress, and giving them the power to keep improving. It's about more than just being fit in the moment; it's about creating a lifetime of active living and wellness.

# 2

# STUDENT GROWTH AND DEVELOPMENT

## Childhood Development Theories

When it comes to understanding how kiddos grow and mature, childhood development theories have got our back. They give us the deets on the physical, cognitive, social, and emotional development of these tiny humans, helping us educators and caregivers support them every step of the way.

Now, hold on tight as we dive headfirst into the world of childhood development theories. Brace yourself because each theory we'll explore offers a unique perspective on how children grow and learn. From the deep thoughts of Sigmund Freud to the wise words of Jean Piaget, we're about to uncover the inner workings of a child's mind.

Let's start with good ol' Freud. This dude believed that our early childhood experiences have a massive impact on how we develop later in life. His psychoanalytic theory is all about those unconscious drives and resolving inner conflicts. According to Freud, kiddos go through different stages called the psychosexual stages, like the oral, anal, and phallic stages. Each stage brings with it its own set of challenges and fixations that can shape who they become as grown-ups.

Moving on from Freud, we've got Mr. Piaget to shake things up a bit. He's all about cognitive development, aka how kids acquire knowledge and make sense of the world around them. According to Piaget, children are like little scientists. They construct their understanding of the world through hands-on exploration and interacting with everything in sight. Piaget said there are four stages of cognitive development: sensorimotor, preoperational, concrete operational, and formal operational stages. He believed that it's crucial to give kids lots of opportunities to problem-solve and think critically.

But it's not all about Freud and Piaget. We've got Lev Vygotsky to bring in a whole new perspective. His sociocultural theory puts social interaction and cultural context front and center. Vygotsky said that kids learn and develop within the context of their social interactions and the kind of environment they're in. He introduced the idea of the "zone of proximal development," which is like a level of tasks and skills that kiddos can handle with a little guidance from a knowledgeable adult or peer. Vygotsky tells us that creating collaborative learning environments and giving kiddos some extra support is where it's at.

And last but definitely not least, we've got Erik Erikson and his psychosocial theory. This dude is all about the connections between internal development and the social environment. Erikson gave us a series of psychosocial stages, each with a unique task or challenge that people need to tackle to have healthy relationships and mental well-being. These stages stretch from baby-days all the way up to old age, and they show us how resolving conflicts and developing a sense of identity and purpose are key parts of a person's growth.

Alrighty, now that we've dipped our toes into some of these childhood development theories, let me tell you that there's a whole lot more where that came from. Seriously, these theories are like a treasure trove of knowledge for us educators and caregivers. They give us the inside scoop on how to create nurturing environments that help kiddos grow and develop in all the best ways possible. If we take these theories to heart and use their principles, we can make sure that our little ones have the best shot at thriving and reaching their full potential.

## Physical Development Milestones

Let me start with the magical beginning of life, when a newborn baby stretches their little arms and legs out into this big ol' world. Those first few months are something else, I tell ya. The baby's reflexes steal the show, mesmerizing us with their curious antics. Take the grasp reflex, for example. It's a heart-melter to see those tiny fingers wrapping around someone's outstretched finger, like a sneak peek at their newfound sense of independence.

But hold onto your hats, folks, 'cause time keeps on truckin', and that baby quickly transforms into a full-blown explorer. Around four months old, they uncover the magic of rolling. It's like they've cracked the code to a whole new world of potential. With a little help from their muscles and bones, they pivot and maneuver their way around, defying gravity with every roll.

And before you know it, that little baby takes their first teetering steps towards freedom. Usually around their first birthday, their loved ones go nuts with excitement as they watch those wobbly legs give it their all. Every step they take is a living testament to their persistence and determination, you know? They stumble, they fall, but they pick themselves back up and keep on moving forward.

As the years go by, that kiddo's physicality evolves right alongside their wild imagination. By the time they hit the ripe ol' age of two, they're on a quest for independence. Suddenly, their limbs are all under control, and they're climbing, running, and jumping like it's nobody's business. Sure, they get a few scrapes and bruises along the way, but that's just a sign of their never-ending thirst for adventure.

And then, whoosh. Here comes adolescence, and the body decides to put on a show. It's like a hidden treasure chest of changes gets cracked open. Puberty hits, and limbs start lengthening, shapes start shifting. It's an all-out transformation. Boys and girls both get to experience the beauty of secondary sexual characteristics, marking the start of a brand spankin' new chapter in their physical development.

As they mosey through those wild teenage years, they start to find their place in the adult world. Their bodies, once shaped by outside forces, kinda take the reins and start maturing on their own terms. Muscles get swole, endurance steps up its game, and physical limits that once seemed impossible get shattered. Every challenge they conquer brings 'em one step closer to fully embracing their own unique grown-up identity.

And finally, we've arrived at the peak of physical development—good ol' adulthood. It's the end result of years and years of growth and transformation. The body, now fully formed and seasoned by time, struts its stuff with a symphony of movements. They push the boundaries, break through limitations, and achieve physical feats that would've seemed downright crazy way back when.

So, as we journey through these mind-blowing milestones of physical development, we're witnesses to the sheer amazingness of the human body. It's a testament to resilience, adaptability, and the relentless pursuit of progress. And so, we keep on truckin', eager to uncover more wonders as we dive deeper into the intricate world of the Praxis Health and Physical Education Content Knowledge 5857 exam. Let the adventure continue!

## Cognitive Development in Children

At Test Treasure Publication, we understand just how important it is to help kids grow their brains. It's like diving into a magnificent maze of thoughts and experiences, exploring all the amazing things happening inside those little heads.

When it comes to cognitive development, kids are like little discoverers. They soak up everything like sponges, growing and learning at lightning speed. Their brains are like busy construction sites, building connections and strengthening synapses, all so they can soak up knowledge and make sense of the world.

But there's more to it than that. Within this world of brainpower, there are different skills that shape how kids think. Paying attention is like the golden ticket, helping them focus on stuff, pick out what's important, and keep their minds on the right track. Whether it's being fascinated by a fun toy, listening with wide eyes to a story, or diving headfirst into imaginative play, attention is like the bridge linking little learners to a sea of knowledge.

And let's not forget about memory. It's like a superhero power that lets kids remember stuff, from a familiar face they've seen before to remembering a whole series of events. Memories are like colorful paintings in their minds, bringing the past to life and giving them access to a treasure trove of knowledge. Through repeated experiences and storing memories, kids build their own bank of understanding, connecting the dots and making sense of the world around them.

Problem-solving is like being a little detective. Kids start piecing things together, figuring out all sorts of puzzles and challenges along the way. It's like building a puzzle, crafting a complex block structure, or even tackling math problems. Their little minds become experts at problem-solving, hungry to unlock all the secrets the world holds.

And don't forget about language development. It's a big deal too. Kids start off with the cutest babblings and coos, slowly but surely conquering the complexities of language. Each word they learn becomes a bridge that connects their thoughts to the wide open world. And as they grow their language skills, kids start expressing themselves, sharing their desires, needs, and endless curiosity. It's like they're building a highway to connect with others, expressing themselves, and gathering all the learning they can.

The journey of cognitive development is fascinating because every child has their own path. They unravel the mysteries of the mind at their own pace, in their own unique way. But at Test Treasure Publication, we're here to help guide and nourish that growth. Our study materials are crafted with care, packed with strategies, tips, and fun activities to join kids in their amazing adventures of learning.

With every page turned, we invite kids to embrace the wonders of thought, to exercise their brains in problem-solving, and to journey towards intellectual growth. Through personalized learning, we want to ignite that love for knowledge, to brighten up their world, and set them on a path to reach for the stars.

So, come along and join us at Test Treasure Publication. Let's dive into the realm of cognitive development in kids and help them become exceptional learners. Together, we'll light their way, as we journey beyond ordinary learning and help them reach for their dreams.

## Social and Emotional Development

Alright, folks, buckle up because we're about to dive deep into the wild world of social development. You see, us humans, we thrive on connections. From the moment we're born, we're wired to form attachments with others. It's like we're hardwired to be social butterflies, fluttering from one connection to another. In this phase of the exploration, we're going to get down and dirty with the stages of social development. We'll witness babies bonding with their caregivers and kids maneuvering through the tricky terrain of peer relationships. Brace yourselves for some captivating stories and mind-blowing analysis as we unravel the secrets behind our social interactions. And hey, we're not just here to unravel, we're here to provide practical strategies to help you actually build healthy and meaningful connections. Now, isn't that a sweet deal?

Now, let's talk emotions. We all know they're a big part of being human. And guess what? They're not just hanging out there for no reason. Nope, emotions are like a superpower that can be honed and mastered. So, in this step of the journey, we're going to dive headfirst into the fascinating world of emotional intelligence. We'll explore the different parts that make up this superhero skill: self-awareness, self-regulation, empathy, and effective communication. Get ready for mind-boggling exercises and real-life examples that will equip you with the tools you need to rock emotional intelligence like a boss. Because trust me, being able to handle your emotions like a pro can seriously level up your personal and professional life.

Now, let's talk resilience. Life, my friends, is a rollercoaster ride of challenges and obstacles. But you know what? Having some resilience in your back pocket can make all the difference. It's like a secret weapon that helps you navigate the ups and downs with grace. In this step, we're going to explore what resilience is all about and why it's so freaking important for your social and emotional development. We'll dive into the factors that contribute to resilience, like having strong personal relationships, getting that growth mindset, and finding healthy ways to cope with whatever life throws at you. And get ready for some seriously inspiring stories of people who have conquered adversity. Their tales will leave you feeling empowered and ready to build up your own resilience, turning challenges into opportunities for personal growth.

Last but certainly not least, let's talk mental health. We all know how crucial it is to keep that delicate balance of social and emotional well-being in check. After all, it's the key to our overall mental health. So, in this final step, we're going to shed light on the connection between social and emotional development and our mental well-being. On this part of the journey, we'll learn all about self-care, showing ourselves a little compassion, and seeking support from trusted folks or professionals when we need it. We'll arm you with comprehensive resources and killer tips to help you make your mental well-being a top priority. Because let's face it, folks, when our mental health is flourishing, everything else just falls into place.

So, my friends, welcome to this chapter on social and emotional development. Get ready to transform your life from the inside out, nurturing your whole self and those around you. Armed with a solid understanding of social development, emotional intelligence, resilience, and the promotion of positive mental health, you'll have all the tools you need to navigate the crazy world of human connection and emotional well-being. Join us on this epic journey of self-discovery and unlock the untapped potential within you. Together, we'll build a foundation for a truly fulfilling and joy-filled existence. Let's do this!

# 3

# MANAGEMENT, MOTIVATION, AND COMMUNICATION

## Classroom Management Techniques

Classroom management techniques. Ah, the ancient art of keeping a bunch of rowdy students in check. It's been around since the dawn of time, as long as people have been seeking knowledge. And let me tell you, it's evolved a lot over the years. Think of it as a dance between different teaching philosophies, educational theories, and the unique dynamics of each classroom. It's like a puzzle, always changing, always challenging.

But to really get it, to really understand what classroom management is all about, we've got to go back in time. Buckle up, my friends, because we're about to embark on a journey through history - where the legends of education come to life and their innovative techniques unfold.

Our first stop? Ancient Greece. Picture this: the wise philosopher Socrates, the OG teacher. He didn't just stand in front of his students and lecture them. No, no. Socrates believed in dialogue, in open inquiry. His Socratic method made his students question everything and engage in deep intellectual conversations. It wasn't just about teaching facts; it was about empowering these young minds to think for themselves, to explore ideas. And let me tell you, it created a unique bond between teacher and student. Talk about effective classroom management.

Now, let's fast forward to the Renaissance. Picture Italy, a time of great thinkers. Enter Vittorino da Feltre. He was all about personalized attention. How cool is that? He believed that every student had different needs, different ways of learning. So, he tailored his instruction to each one of them. That was a game-changer. It was all about the students, putting them at the center of the classroom. Can you imagine? That paved the way for the student-centered approaches we see today.

But the fun wasn't over yet. In the 20th century, we saw some serious change. Maria Montessori and John Dewey were leading the charge. Montessori believed in hands-on learning, letting students explore and discover on their own. It was all about tapping into their natural curiosity. And Dewey? Well, he believed in learning by doing. None of that passive listening and memorizing stuff. He wanted students to get up, get involved, and be an active part of their learning experience.

And here we are, in the 21st century. Technology has taken over, my friends. We've got all these fancy gadgets and online platforms that make learning more interactive and collaborative than ever before. Virtual classrooms, online discussions - it's a whole new world. Classroom management has gone digital, breaking through those traditional boundaries and giving us endless possibilities.

But hold up. Before you dive into all these strategies and techniques, remember this: classroom management is not a one-size-fits-all deal. Nope. Each teacher, with their own teaching style and their own unique students, has to adapt and tweak these techniques to make them work. Flexibility is the name of the game. Adaptability is the key to success.

And let's not forget what it's all about. Classroom management isn't just about keeping things in order. No, no. It's about creating an environment where students feel valued, supported, and inspired to learn. It's about making a difference in these young minds, nurturing their potential and helping them become lifelong learners. So, my dear readers, let's dig deep into the art of teaching. Let's unlock the full potential of our classrooms and create a legacy of learning that lasts a lifetime.

## Motivational Strategies

Motivating ourselves to study and conquer the Praxis exam can feel like climbing Mount Everest, but there are some killer strategies that can help us reach the summit. These strategies aren't just your typical textbook stuff - they tap into our individual learning styles, strengths, and weaknesses. It's all about tailoring our techniques to what works best for us and creating an environment where we're engaged and pumped to learn.

One trick up our sleeves is goal-setting. By setting clear goals that we can actually achieve, we give ourselves a sense of purpose and direction. So, instead of looking at the exam as this huge, overwhelming thing, we can break it down into smaller, manageable tasks. Like, we can set the goal of becoming a master in a specific subject within a certain timeframe. It's not only about feeling accomplished when we reach these goals, but it also helps us keep track of our progress and see how far we've come.

Now here's a secret sauce that keeps our motivation sizzling: feedback and recognition. We all thrive on positive reinforcement and knowing that our hard work doesn't go unnoticed. So, while we're hitting the books, it's awesome to seek feedback from our instructors, classmates, or even online forums. Constructive criticism helps us identify where we need to improve and gives us the guts to face those challenges head-on. And hey, let's not forget to celebrate our milestones along the way. Maybe treat ourselves to some well-deserved ice cream after a study sesh or share our progress with friends and family who've got our backs.

Here's the kicker: collaboration and community engagement. Learning isn't a lonely walk in the park; it's a team sport. When we connect with fellow learners, we feel like we're part of something bigger. We can form study groups or jump into online discussions and exchange ideas, get help when we're stuck, and learn from each other's experiences. Knowing there are people in the same boat as us keeps us motivated and reminds us we're not alone in this wild journey.

But wait, there's more! Variety is the spice of motivation. If we stick to the same ol' study routine every day, we might as well be watching paint dry. Mixing things up with visual aids, hands-on activities, and cool interactive technologies keeps things fresh and exciting. So let's bust out those videos, diagrams, and real-life case studies to make the content come alive and stick in our brains like glue.

At the end of the day, the biggest cheerleaders we have are ourselves. Taking the time to reflect on our progress, embracing our strengths, and admitting our weaknesses helps us stay motivated throughout the entire prep process. By figuring out what really drives us and using strategies that align with our values and goals, we can make big things happen.

So, look, these motivational strategies aren't just some fluff. They're the secret ingredients to our success. By understanding and putting these techniques into play, we can go above and beyond, crush that Praxis exam, and write our names in the record books. Let's dive into this journey armed with the power of motivation and show the world what we're made of.

## Communication Skills for Teachers

Alright, folks, let me tell you something - being in a classroom is like being in a whole different world. It's not just about the boring textbooks and lesson plans. It's all about the art of communication, my friends. When you can connect with your students on a deep level, that's when the real magic happens.

So, as a teacher, let me tell you, effective communication is the key. It's what opens up the floodgates of understanding, sparks curiosity, and creates an environment where learning can thrive. In this chapter, we're gonna dive into the power of communication and how it can really make a difference in getting your students engaged and achieving their best.

We're gonna talk about the core principles of communication, like being clear and empathetic, and really listening to what your students have to say. Plus, we can't forget about all those non-verbal cues, like a friendly smile or a reassuring hand on the shoulder. Trust me, my friends, these little things can make a huge impact on your classroom.

Chapter 2 is all about building rapport with your students. You see, a successful teacher-student relationship starts with a solid foundation of connection. And that connection can lead to collaboration, trust, and a sense of belonging. We're gonna explore how to create that welcoming and inclusive atmosphere where your students feel valued, respected, and heard. Get ready for some icebreaker activities and personalized feedback, my friends, 'cause we're gonna be forging some real connections here.

Now, in chapter 3, we're gonna tackle the art of active listening and empathy. I know, I know, it can be tough with all the chaos and noise in the classroom, but trust me, it's worth it. We're gonna guide you through the process of becoming a compassionate listener who not only hears the words but understands the emotions and needs behind them. We're gonna bridge the gap, my friends, and create a space where everyone feels understood and supported.

And let's not forget about the power of non-verbal communication, my friends. Chapter 4 is all about that. Sometimes, words just aren't enough to convey what we really mean. That's when body language, gestures, and facial expressions come in. We're gonna dive into how you can use these non-verbal cues to shape how your students perceive things and get them engaged and motivated. It's all about creating that positive learning environment, my friends, where every little gesture counts.

Last but not least, chapter 5 is all about conflict resolution and those not-so-easy conversations. Let's face it, guys, conflicts are bound to happen, even in the best classrooms. But don't worry, we've got your back. We're gonna equip you with the skills and strategies to approach those tough situations with fairness, sensitivity, and clear communication. We're talking about de-escalation techniques, active problem-solving, and creating a space where everyone feels like their voice is heard.

So, my friends, keep turning those pages and let this book guide you on your journey to becoming an inspiring and effective communicator in the classroom. There's still so much more to learn, so get ready for more chapters filled with relatable stories, practical advice, and the tools you need to make a real impact on your students' lives. It's gonna be one heck of a ride, my friends. Are you ready?

## Conflict Resolution

Step 1: So, here we are, about to dive into the messy world of conflict resolution. But before we can even think about coming up with solutions, we gotta untangle all the knots of the situation. We need to really define and understand what the conflict is all about. Is it a simple case of coworkers not seeing eye to eye? Or maybe it's a battle of ideas within a team? Heck, it might even be a full-on blowout with a friend or loved one. Whatever it is, we gotta strip away all the layers and get to the real heart of the matter. Once we do that, we're ready to start fixing things.

Step 2: Alright, emotions are about to hit us like a tidal wave. And let's be real, they're gonna mess with our heads and screw up our ability to talk like normal human beings. So, this is when we gotta tap into that emotional intelligence superpower we supposedly have. It means recognizing and understanding our own emotions and also trying to figure out what the other person is feeling. By doing that, we can navigate through the rough waters of conflict without totally losing our cool. We gotta be empathetic, really listen to each other, and find a way to stay in control of our own emotions. It's all about creating an environment where we can actually have a real conversation and understand where the other person is coming from.

Step 3: Alright, so we're in the heat of it now. It's so easy to get caught up in what makes us different from each other. I mean, we're practically wearing those differences like a badge of honor. But guess what? That's not gonna help us solve anything. We gotta find some common ground, people. Look for those things we actually agree on. Maybe we share some goals, or have similar values, or hell, maybe we both just want to win the lottery. The idea is to shift our focus from being at odds with each other to actually working together. It might take some brainstorming, some compromising, or even putting ourselves in the other person's shoes to really get it. But once we find that common ground, things might actually start to make sense.

Step 4: Alright, time for the big one – communication. We can't solve anything if we can't talk it out, right? So, we gotta create a space where we can have those real, honest conversations. That means actually listening to each other, not just waiting for our turn to speak. It means being clear about what we're thinking and feeling without attacking or judging the other person. Our choice of words is important, but so is how we say them, and even how we carry ourselves. We gotta be willing to truly hear the other person's perspective and make them feel heard and understood.

Step 5: Here we are, at the point where we get to come up with some solutions. This is where we get to flex our creative muscles and think outside the box. We gotta throw all our ideas out there and really consider what everyone needs and wants. It's all about finding those win-win solutions that actually address the core of the problem. Sometimes that means compromising, other times it means negotiating, and in some cases, we might need a neutral third party to help us mediate. The point is, we gotta explore all our options and not be afraid to try something unconventional.

Step 6: Alright, we're almost there. We have a solution in mind and now it's time to put it into action. But we can't just call it a day - we gotta stick with it and see if it actually works. That means taking real steps towards implementing it, holding ourselves and others accountable, and keeping those lines of communication open. We gotta check in and see if everything's going as planned, if it's making a difference. And if it's not, then we gotta figure out what needs adjusting and keep at it until we find something that sticks.

Look, I know this whole conflict resolution thing can be a major pain in the ass. But trust me, every conflict is an opportunity for us to grow and learn. It's a chance for us to understand each other better and find some common ground. So, let's embrace the challenges that come our way and keep pushing forward. Together, armed with our newfound knowledge and skills, we can create a world where conflicts aren't scary, but instead, they're stepping stones towards harmony and unity. Let's do this.

# 4

# Planning, Instruction, and Student Assessment

## Curriculum Planning and Design

In this chapter, we're going to dive headfirst into the world of curriculum design. Get ready to explore the art of creating kick-ass learning experiences that actually mean something. But before we get started, we need to do some soul-searching and figure out what the heck we believe about education. Because let's face it, that's where a solid curriculum begins.

First things first, we need to unravel the mysterious puzzle that is curriculum development. We're going to break it down into little pieces and examine how they all fit together. We'll ask ourselves some tough questions about what we want our students to learn and how the heck we're going to make it happen. And oh yeah, we can't forget about those pesky standards that we need to align everything to.

Now, let's talk about curriculum mapping. It might sound boring, but trust me, it's super important. It's all about organizing our content, skills, and ideas in a way that makes sense. We want our students to build on what they already know and understand, so we gotta plan this stuff carefully. And hey, why not throw in some connections between different subjects while we're at it? Let's make this a well-rounded experience.

Next up, let's chat about different ways to teach. We've got to think about all our unique students and what works best for them. We'll dive deep into differentiated instruction, making sure we're meeting everyone's needs and keeping them interested. And of course, we can't ignore the awesome world of educational technology. We'll figure out how to use it to our advantage and make learning even more exciting.

Assessment time! Yup, we gotta talk about it. It's how we measure progress and make decisions about what to do next. We'll explore all the different ways we can assess our students - formative, summative, you name it. And let's not forget about being fair and inclusive. Our curriculum should work for everyone, no matter their background or abilities.

But don't worry, we're not just leaving you with a bunch of theory. We're gonna give you some practical tools and strategies too. We'll throw in some real-life examples and exercises to help you become a curriculum pro. You'll be designing and implementing learning experiences that make your students jump out of bed in the morning.

So get ready for the ride of a lifetime. In this chapter, we're diving into the world of curriculum planning and design. It's time to unleash your inner curriculum architect and create some seriously awesome learning opportunities. Let's show the world just how extraordinary education can be.

## Instructional Strategies

So, picture this: you're sitting in a classroom, surrounded by a sea of desks and eager students. The teacher walks in, armed with a toolkit of instructional strategies. But here's the thing -- they're not just any old strategies. These babies pack a punch. They're designed to grab your attention, keep you engaged, and help you learn like a boss.

First up, we've got direct instruction. Now, I know what you're thinking -- it sounds pretty old school. And yeah, it is. But don't underestimate the power of the classics. With direct instruction, the teacher takes charge, leading the way and breaking things down step by step. It's like having a tour guide in the world of learning. They make sure you get the basics down before diving into the deep end. Believe me, it's a game-changer.

Next, we've got cooperative learning. Now this one's all about teamwork. Imagine your classroom turning into a hub of collaboration and creativity. You're not just learning from your teacher anymore -- you're learning from your classmates too. Group work, discussions, and projects become the norm, helping you develop those oh-so-important social skills while actually understanding what the heck is going on. It's like a masterclass in productive chaos.

Now, brace yourself for problem-based learning. This one's a doozy. It's like solving a real-life puzzle, except the pieces are made up of complex, juicy problems. You're challenged to think outside the box, apply your knowledge, and come up with creative solutions. It's like diving headfirst into the real world, where nothing is handed to you on a silver platter. You've got to roll up your sleeves and get your hands dirty. Trust me though, it's totally worth it.

Alright, let's talk about differentiated instruction. We all know not every student is the same. We've all got our strengths and weaknesses, our likes and dislikes. And that's where differentiated instruction comes in. It's all about tailoring the learning experience to meet your unique needs. You get a personalized roadmap to success, with different assignments, grouping options, and even individual learning plans. It's like having a classroom that's custom-made just for you.

Last but not least, we've got technology integration. Yeah, we're in the digital age, my friend. Technology isn't just a distraction anymore -- it's a powerful tool for learning. Imagine interactive presentations, online simulations, and educational apps making your lessons come alive. It's like stepping into a whole new dimension of learning, where anything is possible. Just remember, with great power comes great responsibility. Digital literacy and responsible use of technology are key, my friend.

Now, here's a little secret: these strategies aren't meant to be used in isolation. A skilled educator knows how to blend them together, like a master chef creating a culinary masterpiece. They choose the right strategies for the right moment, based on what you need and what the content demands. It's a delicate dance, but when it's done right, it creates a magical learning experience that propels you towards success.

So, my friend, let's embark on this epic journey together. We'll unearth the treasures of instructional strategies, discovering their transformative power within the walls of our classrooms. Get ready to be amazed, inspired, and empowered. Your learning adventure starts now.

## Formative and Summative Assessments

Imagine walking through a dense forest, with every step revealing new wonders and mysteries. That's what learning feels like, an adventure full of surprises and discoveries. And just like in that forest, formative assessments are like signposts along the way, showing us how far we've come and how much further we can go. They come in all shapes and sizes, from class discussions to online quizzes, and they give us a chance to reflect on our progress and figure out where we need to focus our efforts.

But don't think of formative assessments as the end of the road. Oh no, there's still more to come. Summative assessments are like towering mountains, challenging us to prove our mastery of the subject. They're the ultimate test, where we get to show off everything we've learned. It's like reaching the peak of a magnificent summit after facing countless obstacles. That feeling of triumph, of knowing that you've conquered the hardest challenges, that's what summative assessments are all about.

Now, when you think of summative assessments, you might imagine those high-stakes exams that we all dread. But they can also be projects, portfolios, or presentations, giving us a chance to show our knowledge in a more creative way. The results of these assessments carry a lot of weight, because they can shape our future opportunities. They can open doors for us or close them, depending on how well we perform.

Formative and summative assessments are like dance partners, moving together in perfect harmony. They're not separate events, but connected phases of our learning journey. Formative assessments guide us along the way, giving us feedback and support. And summative assessments mark the grand finale, where we get to showcase our growth and celebrate our achievements.

As educators, it's our job to use both formative and summative assessments to create the best possible learning experience. With formative assessments, we can offer timely feedback and guidance, helping our students reach their full potential. And with summative assessments, we can see the bigger picture, understanding their overall growth and readiness for what's to come.

But let's not forget that formative and summative assessments are more than just grades or scores on a report card. They represent our journey of transformation and growth. Together, let's embrace the power of these assessments, unlocking the potential within each and every student. Because when we do, we open the doors to endless possibilities and create a brighter future for all.

So keep your eyes peeled, because we're about to dive into the nitty-gritty of formative and summative assessments. We'll explore all the specific strategies and techniques to make these evaluations work for us. Together, we can unleash the true power of education and make a real difference in the lives of our students.

## Feedback Mechanisms

1. Let's start by figuring out what gets our bodies going - the stimulus. Picture yourself under the blazing sun on a scorching summer day. You can practically feel those sun rays burning into your skin. That intense heat sets off a chain reaction within us, making our bodies kick into action to maintain their balance - what we like to call homeostasis.

2. This is where our incredible sensors come in. They're like superheroes embedded throughout our bodies, always on the lookout for any changes in our surroundings. When it comes to the heat, these sensors pick up on the rising temperature and send signals to the control center of our body.

3. The control center, nestled somewhere in our brain or spinal cord, receives these signals like it's getting important messages. It's basically the boss in charge, orchestrating how our body will respond. In our case, it's getting the memo about the heat and getting ready for action.

4. Now, here's the really cool part. The control center sets things in motion by sending signals through our nervous system or even our endocrine system. These signals act like messengers, zooming around and traveling at lightning speed to our effectors - the organs or tissues ready to respond.

5. Our effectors are like finely-tuned instruments, playing the control center's instructions to perfection. In the heat situation, imagine our sweat glands taking center stage. They start pumping out fluid onto our skin, creating a cool sensation as it evaporates. This response is what keeps our body temperature in check, preventing us from overheating and keeping us in tip-top shape.

6. Thanks to this intricate feedback system, our body finds its balance again and returns to its state of homeostasis. The rise in temperature triggered a whole series of events that ultimately led to the cooling response, effectively cancelling out the initial stimulus. This delicate dance, made possible by feedback mechanisms, ensures that our bodies work like a well-oiled machine, even when facing tough conditions.

As we dive into the world of Praxis Health and Physical Education, we begin to truly appreciate the wonder of feedback mechanisms. They're like hidden heroes, tirelessly working behind the scenes to maintain our body's equilibrium and keep us in sync with our surroundings. Through these mechanisms, our bodies become a symphony of connections and resilience.

So, let's embrace the marvels of feedback mechanisms and acknowledge their power to adapt, regulate, and safeguard our bodies. As we understand these mechanisms, we gain a deep understanding of our own inner workings and arm ourselves with tools to take care of our well-being. With each step, we approach Praxis with confidence, armed with knowledge and a deep admiration for the intricate symphony of our own physiology.

# 5

# COLLABORATION, REFLECTION, AND TECHNOLOGY

## Teamwork and Collaboration in Education

Alright, folks, buckle up because we're about to dive into the ins and outs of teamwork and collaboration in education. Trust me, this stuff is important, and by the end of this chapter, you'll see why.

First things first, we gotta establish some clear goals. I mean, how can we expect to work together if we don't know what we're working towards, right? As educators, it's our job to make sure everyone is on the same page and understands the vision. When we lay out those goals and communicate them effectively, we give our team a sense of purpose and direction.

Next up, we gotta build an environment that supports collaboration. We want people to feel comfortable and valued when they're working with us. That means we need to create space for open dialogue, active listening, and the exchange of ideas. When we embrace diversity and inclusivity, we're setting the stage for a truly collaborative culture.

Now, let's talk about active participation. This is the secret sauce to effective teamwork. In the classroom, we can foster active participation by getting students involved in the learning process. Think interactive teaching methods and group activities that encourage students to engage with each other and the material.

When we give students the opportunity to take on different roles and be responsible for their own learning, we're lighting that fire of ownership and accountability.

We can't forget about communication. It's the beating heart of any successful team. In education, that means establishing clear channels of communication between teachers, students, administrators, and parents. And it's not just about talking. We've gotta be good listeners too. Seeking feedback, addressing concerns, and being open and transparent with our communication creates an atmosphere of trust and understanding.

Now, here's where things get really exciting - interdisciplinary collaboration. We're living in a connected world, people, and we need to prepare our students for that. By encouraging collaboration across different subjects and disciplines, we're exposing them to diverse perspectives and fostering critical thinking and creativity. And hey, it's not just the students who benefit - us educators can learn a thing or two from collaborating with our colleagues too.

Okay, time to assess and reflect on our teamwork. We can't improve if we don't know how we're doing, right? So let's incorporate assessments that specifically evaluate teamwork skills. This encourages students to think about their contributions, strengths, and areas for growth. And it's not just the students who need to reflect - us teachers have to step back and consider how we can enhance collaboration in the classroom too.

And there you have it, folks. When we embrace teamwork and collaboration in education, we create an environment where our students can thrive academically, socially, and emotionally. It's all about empowering our learners to reach their potential in a world where collaboration is the name of the game. So let's embark on this journey together and discover the incredible power of teamwork and collaboration in education.

# Reflective Teaching Practices

Step 1: Self-Reflection

Alright, so the first thing we gotta do is some serious self-reflection. Take a moment to really think about how you teach, how you run your classroom, and the strategies you use. We're talking deep stuff here. Think about what you're good at and what areas could use some work. This is gonna set the groundwork for some major growth, so take your time with it.

Step 2: Seeking Feedback

Now here's the fun part. We gotta start asking for some feedback from others. This could be your colleagues, your students, or even your friends and family. Get different perspectives, ya know? Maybe have a peer come in and observe your class, or hand out some surveys to the students. Be open to criticism, because that's how we grow.

Step 3: Analysis and Evaluation

Once you've gathered all that feedback, it's time to really dig in and analyze it. Look for any patterns or trends in what people are saying about your teaching. Figure out where you need to make some changes. And let's not be afraid to get real critical here, alright? We gotta take a hard look at ourselves and our teaching methods.

Step 4: Setting Goals

Based on all that self-reflection and feedback, it's time to set some goals for yourself. And not just any goals, we're talking SMART goals. Specific, measurable, attainable, relevant, and time-bound. Make 'em clear and actionable. And don't keep 'em to yourself, share 'em with your colleagues and mentors who can help keep you on track.

Step 5: Experimentation and Reflection

Now comes the fun part - time to try out some new teaching strategies. Get out of your comfort zone a bit, you know? Try different things and see what works. And don't forget to keep reflecting on how these changes are impacting your students. Be willing to tweak things as you go.

Step 6: Collaboration and Professional Development

You can't do this reflective teaching thing all by yourself. It's all about collaboration and ongoing learning. Talk to your fellow teachers, share ideas and strategies. Go to workshops and conferences to stay up to date with the latest research. The more you put yourself out there, the more you'll grow as a teacher.

Step 7: Continuous Improvement

Alright, we're at the last step but it's definitely not the end. Reflective teaching is a journey, my friend. There's no finish line. Keep revisiting your goals, assess how you're doing, and make any necessary adjustments. Embrace change and be flexible with your teaching methods. We're always learning and growing, so let's keep at it, alright?

Incorporating reflective teaching practices into your approach has the power to totally transform your teaching game. Seriously, it can have a profound impact on your students' learning. So get ready to discover some things about yourself and experience some major growth in your professional life. It's gonna be a wild ride, but trust me, it's worth it. Welcome to the club of reflective teachers!

## Technology Integration in Physical Education

Alright, folks, let's dive into this chapter and explore how we can bring technology into the physical education curriculum. We're talking about seamlessly integrating tech into our workouts, but hey, it's not all sunshine and rainbows. We gotta be ready for the challenges that might come our way. So, buckle up, and let's weigh the pros and cons to make this tech integration truly effective and meaningful.

Now, one of the coolest things about using technology in physical education is how it can get our students pumped up and get them actively involved in their own learning. Picture this: kids strapping on virtual reality headsets and being transported back in time to ancient Greece. They're not just exploring history, but they're also taking part in virtual sports competitions. Talk about a double whammy! It's like hitting two birds with one stone, you know? We got engaging activities and a sick way to learn about history and culture.

And that's not all! Technology can also help us personalize learning and assessment in PE. I'm talking about wearables, like fitness trackers and heart rate monitors, that allow students to track their progress in real-time. They get that instant feedback, which pushes them to go harder. Plus, us teachers can analyze all that data and tailor our instruction to meet each student's unique needs. It's like customizing education for every student, and that's a game-changer.

Now, let's not forget, it's not all smooth sailing when it comes to integrating technology into PE. We gotta make sure everyone has access to the tech goodies. Some schools have all the resources, but others might be struggling to provide equal opportunities. It's on us to find creative solutions, like securing grants or collaborating with local groups, to make sure all our students can get their hands on the tech tools that make our classes epic.

Another thing we gotta keep in mind is that technology should never overshadow the real heart and soul of physical education. Yeah, it's cool to have all these gadgets, but we should always remember that our focus is on promoting health, wellness, and physical activity. We need to strike a balance between using technology and giving our students plenty of chances to get active, develop their skills, and interact with each other.

In the next sections, we'll dig even deeper and explore specific examples of how technology can amp up our PE classes. We'll talk about apps, websites, and devices that can make our instruction more engaging and get our students pumped up for real physical activities. We'll also share some strategies for tackling those challenges that might pop up along the way. Trust me, we've got your back.

Folks, by embracing the power of technology, we can create a PE environment that's exciting, inclusive, and transformative. We're embarking on this journey together, and our endgame is to equip our students with the knowledge, skills, and attitudes they need for a lifetime of health and wellness. With each step we take, we light up the path to success, where technology and physical education join forces to shape the future of our incredible students.

## Professional Development Resources

Hey there, fellow educators! Looking to take your teaching game to the next level? Well, you've come to the right place. Our professional development resources are like a treasure trove of tools and materials that will supercharge your effectiveness in the classroom.

Picture this - comprehensive study guides that dig deep into the core concepts of health and physical education. It's like having a solid foundation that allows you to build something truly amazing. And we're not just talking about dry, boring content here. These guides are all about real-life scenarios and practical applications. We're bridging that pesky gap between theory and practice, my friend.

But we're not stopping there. Interactive online resources are the name of the game. We've got all sorts of cool stuff to keep you engaged and collaborating with fellow educators. Think interactive quizzes that make learning a breeze. Imagine discussion forums where you can bounce ideas off each other. And how about virtual workshops led by the pros themselves? It's like a party for teachers, but with a purpose.

We know that each and every one of you is unique, so we're all about personalizing your learning experience. We want to empower you to take charge of your own growth. That's why we offer personalized learning plans that are tailored to your specific needs and goals. Whether you're a seasoned pro who wants to dive deeper into your expertise or a newbie who needs some guidance, we've got your back. Consider us your personal roadmap to success.

But wait, there's more! We understand that learning doesn't just happen inside the four walls of a classroom. That's why we offer experiential learning opportunities that take you beyond the traditional. Imagine getting hands-on experience through internships and mentorship programs. It's like stepping out into a whole new world. Not only will you enhance your knowledge and skills, but you'll also make valuable connections within the field. It's a win-win situation, my friend.

We're not ones to stay in the past. We're constantly on the lookout for the latest research and trends in health and physical education. That's why our professional development resources are regularly updated to reflect the cutting-edge stuff. We collaborate with the best of the best to make sure our materials are on point, accurate, and aligned with the current standards and best practices. We've got our finger on the pulse of education, so you know you're getting the good stuff.

Here's the thing, my fellow educators. Professional development isn't just a checkbox to tick off. It's a lifelong journey towards excellence. We're here to inspire and empower you on that journey. We want to nurture your passion and help you soar to new heights in your career. So, come join us on this mission of continuous learning and professional growth. Let's unlock the potential within ourselves and our students, together. Are you in?

# 6

# HEALTH EDUCATION AS A DISCIPLINE

## Introduction to Health Education

Let me tell you about this incredible journey we're embarking on together. It's not just about cramming our brains with facts and figures about health; it's about something much bigger. It's about giving you the power to take control of your own well-being and make informed choices that will light up your life with vitality, balance, and fulfillment.

In this chapter, we're diving deep into the heart of health education and how it has evolved over time. We're going to explore how your physical, mental, and emotional health are all intertwined and shape your overall well-being.

Forget about waiting for something to go wrong before doing something about it. That's not what this journey is about. It's all about equipping you with the tools you need to maintain your health throughout your life. It's about being proactive and spotting those risk factors, and then adopting positive habits that make your body and mind thrive.

But here's the thing: to make this journey truly successful, your educators need to get to know you. They need to understand where you come from and what makes you tick. In this chapter, we're going to dive into the world of culturally responsive teaching, where we celebrate your unique perspectives and experiences that shape your own beliefs about health.

And you know what? We're not just stopping there. We're going to explore how health education can bring all of us together, creating inclusive communities where everyone has access to the resources and knowledge they need for a healthy and fulfilling life. It's about fairness and justice, my friend. Everyone deserves a shot at a better life, and we're going to make it happen.

We're also going to take a good, hard look at how technology is changing the game when it comes to health education. Gone are the days of boring textbooks. We're talking about interactive platforms and educational apps that bring learning to life and boost your health knowledge.

But wait, there's more! We're also going to talk about the power of collaboration and community partnerships in this journey of ours. By working together with your family, healthcare professionals, and community organizations, we can create a solid support system that's got your back every step of the way.

So, my friend, get ready to dive into the world of health education with me. It's a big responsibility, but together we can unleash the transformative power of knowledge. With your newfound understanding, you'll be able to take control of your health and make a difference in your community. Let's embark on this eye-opening adventure where gaining knowledge goes hand in hand with building a healthier and happier world.

## Health Promotion Theories

Step 1: Understanding the Foundations

Alright, let's kick things off with the nitty-gritty. In this first step, we're diving deep into the theoretical foundations of health promotion. I'm talking about the stuff that lays the groundwork for everything we're gonna learn. So buckle up.

The first thing we're gonna focus on is the socioecological model. This bad boy is all about how everything is connected when it comes to health. We're talkin' individuals, their environments, and all the different factors that shape how people behave when it comes to their health. This model shows us that health promotion ain't just some one-size-fits-all deal. It's a whole package deal that needs interventions that cover all the bases - from individuals, to communities, to society at large.

Step 2: The Health Belief Model

Next up on our trip through health promotion theories, we've got the Health Belief Model. This one gets up close and personal with how individuals perceive their own health. We're talking about how they see their susceptibility to certain health issues, how severe they think those issues are, and what they believe are the benefits of takin' action or the barriers holdin' 'em back. It's all about people's perceptions and how they weigh the risks and rewards before makin' changes in their lives.

Step 3: The Transtheoretical Model

Moving along, we're entering the world of the Transtheoretical Model, also known as the Stages of Change model. This one tells us that behavior change ain't some overnight thing. It's a journey, my friend. People go through different stages - from not even thinkin' about change, to contemplatin' it, to preparin' for it, to taking actual action, and so on. By gettin' a handle on these stages and the processes that come with 'em, we can craft interventions that meet folks wherever they're at in their journey towards healthier habits.

Step 4: Social Cognitive Theory

Now it's time to check out the Social Cognitive Theory. This theory tells us that behavior change is influenced by a whole buncha things - personal factors, how people behave, their environment, and even their own belief in their ability to make changes, aka self-efficacy. We gotta understand how all these factors interact and impact people's health behaviors. By doin' that, we can create interventions that actually empower individuals to take charge and make healthier choices.

Step 5: The Diffusion of Innovations Theory

Alright, folks. We're at our final stop on this wild ride through health promotion theories. Here, we're divin' into the Diffusion of Innovations Theory. This one shows us how new ideas, behaviors, and technologies spread through society. We wanna know what makes people jump on board with new ways of doin' things and what holds 'em back. Understanding these factors helps us promote and implement evidence-based interventions that can actually make a difference in people's lives.

So there you have it, mates. This step-by-step guide is gonna take you on a journey through the ins and outs of health promotion theories. You're gonna see how all these different theories fit together and get a deeper understanding of what makes people tick when it comes to their health. And remember, this ain't just a map we're givin' ya. We're here by your side, helpin' ya navigate the twists and turns, and showin' ya the way to success in your studies. So get ready, 'cause we're about to embark on a journey that'll shape a healthier future for all of us. Let's do this!

## Ethics in Health Education

Let me take you back to the ancient days, where it all began. Picture this: the bustling civilizations of Greece and Rome, filled with people thirsty for knowledge and hungry to understand the human body. These folks set the foundation for the ethical principles that would shape health education for years to come. We're talking philosophers like Hippocrates and Galen, who not only added to medical knowledge, but also stressed the importance of ethical conduct in medicine and health education.

Fast forward to the Middle Ages, and you can bet your bottom dollar that religious institutions had a big say in health education ethics. Those religious teachings instilled in us the values of compassion, care, and respect for life, shaping the way health educators approached their profession. The monks and nuns of the time played a major role, providing care and education, cherishing both physical and spiritual well-being.

Now, let's dive into the Renaissance period. This was a time of discovery and scientific breakthroughs, and boy, did it propel health education forward. Ethical considerations expanded to include things like informed consent, patient autonomy, and the duty to educate folks on making healthy choices. The Renaissance humanists were all about empowering individuals with knowledge and giving them a voice in their own healthcare decisions.

Flash forward to the 19th and 20th centuries, and you'll see massive changes in the healthcare system that had health educators scratching their heads. Public health took the stage, medical research boomed, and suddenly, ethical challenges were popping up left and right. Issues of privacy, fairness, and balancing individual rights with public health interests were thrown their way. To keep up with it all, professional organizations and associations stepped up to the plate, creating codes of ethics to guide health educators and maintain top-notch conduct.

So where are we now? Well, my friend, it's the present day, and things are changing at lightning speed. With the rise of digital health platforms, big data usage, and telehealth integration, health educators are finding themselves lost in a sea of new ethical dilemmas. Privacy, data security, and fair access to healthcare resources have become the big issues in this ever-changing landscape.

With all these ethical considerations buzzing around, it's crucial for folks like us in the health education field to walk a fine line. We need to balance individual autonomy with the greater good of society. And let me tell you, it's no easy task. But we've got to navigate through it all with sensitivity, empathy, and a rock-solid dedication to the highest ethical standards. Our role isn't just to hand out information; it's about empowering people to make informed decisions, fighting for health equity, and looking out for the well-being of our communities.

Now that you've got a taste of the ethical journey we're on, get ready to dive even deeper. We're going to explore specific ethical principles, dilemmas, and frameworks that guide our practice. By truly understanding these ethics in a reflective way, we'll be ready to tackle the complexities of our profession and become true guardians and advocates for health education ethics in our society.

## Community and Public Health

Let's talk about Community and Public Health. It's this whole big thing, you know? It's not just about being disease-free, but also about being physically, mentally, and socially well. We're talking about a community where people are thriving in every way, where they're supported and empowered to live their best lives.

It's a huge field, with so many factors that affect community well-being. We've got social aspects like income, education, and access to healthcare, and then there are environmental factors like air and water quality, housing conditions, and safety. It's about how all these things connect and play off each other, and it helps us figure out what areas need attention and help.

And then there's this big thing called health equity that we can't ignore. It's all about making sure everyone, no matter who they are or where they come from, has the same chance at being healthy. It's about acknowledging the disparities and unfairness in health outcomes for different groups of people. We've got to look at the bigger picture and recognize the barriers that are keeping some people from getting the care they deserve. We have to work towards tearing those barriers down and creating a more fair and equal society.

But Community and Public Health isn't just about individual communities. It goes beyond that. It's about looking at the health of whole populations. It doesn't matter where you are in the world, we're all in this together. We're talking about epidemiology, biostatistics, the environment, and health policies. We need to understand this stuff so we can tackle the health challenges that affect all of us.

But here's the thing, it's not enough to just understand all this. We've got to put it into action. We need to come up with strategies and interventions that will make communities stronger and healthier. We're talking about things like health education and promotion, and creating programs and policies that support public health. And here's the kicker, we can't do it alone. Change happens when we all come together, individuals, organizations, and communities, and work towards a common goal.

So, are you ready for this journey? It's not just about studying from a book, it's about making a difference in the real world. Let's go out there armed with knowledge, passion, and the belief that we can create a future where everyone is healthier and happier.

# 7

# HEALTH EDUCATION CONTENT

## Nutrition and Healthy Eating Habits

You know, in this crazy modern world we live in, it's so easy to let nutrition take a backseat. Our busy schedules and the allure of convenience often lead us straight to those fast food joints and processed snacks. We sacrifice our health just for a quick and easy meal, not realizing the detrimental effects it can have on our bodies and minds.

But let me tell you something, friend. The significance of nutrition and healthy eating habits goes way beyond just getting by. It's a complex dance between the food we eat and the amazing machine that is our body. Every single thing we put into our mouths plays a crucial role in how our cells, organs, and systems function. Carbs give us energy, proteins help build and repair, and vitamins and minerals keep everything ticking.

And it's not just about what we eat, but how we eat it too. Mindful eating is all about being present and truly connecting with our bodies. It's listening to those hunger cues, savoring each bite, and being mindful of portion sizes. When we take the time to nourish ourselves in a mindful way, we can prevent overeating and emotional eating. We take control of our relationship with food and treat our bodies with the respect they deserve.

With so many fad diets and conflicting information out there, it's so important to get the facts straight. We need to separate the truth from the myths and really understand our food choices. Armed with knowledge, we can make informed decisions that prioritize our health and well-being.

So let's talk about healthy eating habits, shall we? It's not about sticking to strict rules or depriving ourselves. It's about bringing in a variety of whole, nutrient-packed foods that not only nourish our bodies but also bring us pleasure. Think fruits, veggies, whole grains, lean proteins, and healthy fats. By creating a well-rounded plate, we ensure that we're getting all the good stuff our bodies need.

And here's something you might not have realized – nutrition and healthy eating habits have a profound impact on our mental and emotional well-being too. Research shows that a diet rich in nutrients can boost our brain power, improve our mood, and even lower the risk of mental health disorders. It's like a happy pill in every bite. By taking care of our bodies through what we eat, we can achieve clarity, focus, and emotional stability.

So, in the section of this study guide, we're going to dive deep into the nitty-gritty of nutrition and healthy eating habits. We'll explore each food group, their specific nutrients, and how they contribute to our overall health. We'll also talk about the importance of staying hydrated, the benefits of meal planning, and even some tips for making sustainable changes.

But here's the thing – this journey to optimal nutrition and healthy eating isn't just about the facts and figures. It's about truly caring for ourselves and discovering our own unique needs. We need to embrace a holistic approach to wellness and understand that what we put into our bodies affects every single aspect of our lives. So, let's go on this incredible journey together, uncovering the secrets of nutrition and revealing the power of healthy eating habits. It's going to be life-changing.

## Physical Activity and Wellness

Step 1: Understanding the Importance of Physical Activity

Alright, folks, let's get real. When it comes to living our best lives, physical activity is the absolute foundation. We're not just talking about a quick burst of energy or some mindless exercise to fit in with what society expects. No, physical activity is so much more than that. It's like having a magic key that unlocks a world full of health, vitality, and a longer shot at life. Think of it as a beautiful dance with our bodies, where we're nourishing them with movement and setting our spirits free. It's not just about getting a healthy heart or sharpening our minds. Physical activity is the key that unlocks personal growth, self-expression, and a chance to truly discover ourselves.

Step 2: Unveiling the Science of Exercise

Alright, folks, now we're going on a journey into the science of exercise. Get ready to dive deep into the mechanics of human movement, the crazy things our bodies do, and the amazing ways it all affects our physical, mental, and emotional well-being. We're talking about the incredible world of exercise physiology, biomechanics, and energy systems. Trust me, it's mind-blowing. You're gonna see just how our bodies adapt and change when we engage in purposeful movement. It's like a hidden superpower that we all have, waiting to be unleashed.

Step 3: Nurturing Our Bodies with Proper Nutrition

Now, let's get down to the nitty-gritty of taking care of our bodies from the inside out. You see, when we're busting our butts with exercise, our bodies need some serious nutrition to keep up. So, let's explore the wonders of proper nutrition together. We're gonna understand the role of macros, micros, and hydration in maximizing our performance and keeping our health in check. It's like unraveling the mysteries of fueling our bodies for victory. From pre-workout snacks to post-workout meals, and even just our everyday eating habits, we're gonna learn how to create a symphony of nourishment that fuels our bodies and sets our spirits on fire.

Step 4: Cultivating Mental Fortitude and Emotional Well-Being

Alright, now it's time to tap into the power of our minds. You see, physical activity isn't just about the physical. It's a chance to build mental toughness and take care of our emotional well-being too. We're gonna dive deep into mindset training, stress management, and self-care. It's like discovering the connection between our mental well-being and kicking butt in our physical pursuits. We're gonna learn strategies to empower ourselves, build resilience, and face the challenges that come our way on this journey. Trust me, movement is gonna be your partner in self-discovery, self-expression, and becoming the best version of yourself.

Step 5: Designing Personalized Physical Activity Programs

Alright, last but definitely not least, we're gonna talk about designing a program that's as unique as you are. We're all different, right? So our bodies crave different kinds of movement, different levels of intensity, and a plan that's tailor-made for us. We're gonna explore the art of designing personalized physical activity programs. We'll talk about setting goals, finding the right mix of exercises, and integrating all sorts of different training methods. From functional fitness to cardio to strength training, we've got it all covered. Oh, and don't forget about the importance of rest and recovery too. This is your chance to create a blueprint for your own journey to physical activity and wellness. It's all about finding what you love, what you're capable of, and what makes you feel alive.

So there you have it, folks! This chapter on Physical Activity and Wellness is here to show you just how movement can transform your life. It's all about embracing a lifestyle that cherishes and nourishes your body. With a little bit of science, a lot of mental fortitude, and a program that's uniquely yours, you'll set off on a journey of self-discovery and endless potential. So, are you ready to unearth the treasures hidden within your body and unlock the door to a life filled with vibrant health and all-around well-being? I know I am, and I'd love for you to join me on this exhilarating expedition!

## Mental and Emotional Health

When it comes to mental and emotional health, we're diving into the fascinating worlds of our own minds. Our thoughts have this incredible power to shape how we see things and what we do. It's crazy how our self-esteem, self-confidence, and overall well-being are all affected by how we perceive ourselves and our abilities. So, here's the thing - if we want to have a healthy and empowering relationship with ourselves, we need to take a good look at the thoughts dancing around inside our heads.

Alright, let's talk about emotions. They're like a wild ocean, constantly moving and changing. We ride these waves of feeling, going through ups and downs that really influence how we see the world and how we react. It's important to understand the depth of our emotions, whether it's the little ripples of happiness or the crazy storms of sadness and anger. When we get a handle on our emotions, we can navigate through our feelings with grace and self-awareness.

But here's the thing - mental and emotional health doesn't just depend on what's going on inside our heads. It's a delicate balance between what's happening inside us and what's happening outside in the big wide world. Our relationships, our environment, and our experiences all have a hand in our mental and emotional well-being. Building positive relationships and having a supportive group of people around us gives us the strength and resilience we need to deal with life's challenges and celebrate the good stuff.

This whole mental and emotional health thing? It's a lifelong journey, like this beautiful symphony of self-discovery, healing, and growth. We need to commit to it, be kind to ourselves, and be willing to face the uncomfortable stuff that comes up as we explore who we really are. It's like stripping off layer after layer, revealing the vulnerable parts of ourselves and embracing the incredible strength that's hidden within.

So, in this chapter, we're going to dive deep into the ins and outs of mental and emotional health. We'll explore different strategies and techniques to boost our resilience, emotional intelligence, and overall well-being. From practicing mindfulness and being present in the moment to reshaping the way we think with cognitive-behavioral stuff, there's a whole range of possibilities out there for us to try.

So, let's do this, dear reader. Let's go on this amazing journey into our minds and emotions. We'll uncover all the deep complexities and mysterious bits that make us who we are. And together, we'll walk hand in hand towards a future where we're strong, empowered, and filled with endless joy.

## Substance Abuse Education

Let's talk about substance abuse. We all know it's a complicated topic, but it's important to understand what it really means. Substance abuse is basically when someone misuses or uses way too much alcohol, prescription drugs, illegal drugs, or tobacco. And let me tell you, it can have some serious consequences on a person's body, mind, and social life. It's a whole range of behaviors, from just trying it out once in a while to being totally dependent on it all the time.

Now, when it comes to Substance Abuse Education, we gotta get familiar with this three-part deal: prevention, intervention, and treatment. Prevention is all about coming up with smart strategies to promote healthy choices and lower the risk factors for substance abuse. Think things like teaching people about it, getting the community involved, and running programs that help people bounce back and make better decisions.

Intervention is when we gotta step in and help those who are already caught up in substance abuse. We need to spot those at risk, give them the right help, and make sure they have support systems in place to get better. That can mean anything from therapy to finding them the right services to get them back on their feet, you know?

As we dive deep into Substance Abuse Education, we can't ignore the fact that different substances can mess us up in different ways. I'm talking about stuff like alcohol, which is the popular choice for a lot of teens and adults. But we can't forget about drugs like marijuana, cocaine, opioids, and stimulants. Each one comes with its own set of risks and challenges. Oh, and we can't turn a blind eye to the prescription drug problem either. That stuff has been getting more and more out of control lately, and we need to be on high alert.

To really help educators be effective in tackling substance abuse, we gotta understand the psychology, the culture, and the biology behind it all. Things like peer pressure, family dynamics, cultural norms, and mental health stuff - they all play a role. Knowing how substance abuse affects our brains and the long-term consequences is key to giving people the full picture.

And let me tell you, this substance abuse world is always changing. We gotta keep up with the latest research, trends, and best practices. This study guide is gonna give you all the info you need, but it's also gonna make you think, reflect, and analyze. It's gonna get you ready to take action in a smart and informed way.

At Test Treasure Publication, we believe education can change lives. Substance Abuse Education isn't just about giving people facts, it's about giving them the power to build a healthier, stronger future. So let's go on this journey together, let's go beyond the ordinary and embrace the extraordinary. 'Cause when we combine knowledge with action, success is within reach.

## Sexual Health Education

1: Understanding Sexual Health

Welcome, my friends, to the wild and wonderful world of sexual health. Buckle up, because we're about to embark on a journey that'll leave you stunned and breathless. We're diving headfirst into this electric realm, exploring the vibrant dimensions that make up our sexual well-being. So get ready to unravel the puzzle that connects our physical, emotional, and social selves. We won't rest until we've explored every nook and cranny, leaving no stone unturned.

2: Unveiling the Myths

Ah, misinformation, the sneaky snake in the garden of sexual health. It's time to cut through the smoke and mirrors, my friends, and tackle these pesky myths head-on. We'll dig deep into topics like virginity, sexually transmitted infections, and contraception, dispelling the nonsense and giving you the real deal. It's time to arm yourself with accurate knowledge so you can make informed decisions and strut through life like the boss you are.

3: Promoting Healthy Relationships

Let's face it, folks, healthy relationships are the holy grail of sexual well-being. So, in this chapter, we're going all-in on communication, consent, and boundary-setting. We'll shine a spotlight on the intricate dance of respect and equality that lays the foundation for incredible connections. You'll learn how to handle those tricky power dynamics, resolve conflicts like a pro, and build intimacy that'll make your heart sing. Get ready to cultivate relationships founded on trust, understanding, and empathy. It's the recipe for some next-level goodness, my friends.

4: Navigating Consent

Ah, consent, the crucial ingredient in the recipe of sexual interactions. It's time to get real and delve into the many layers of consent. We're giving you a comprehensive guide, complete with engaging scenarios and thought-provoking discussions. By the time we're done here, you'll be equipped with all the tools you need to navigate the wild, wonderful world of consent. You'll become a boundary-setting champion, making informed choices about your body and relationships like the boss you truly are.

5: Contraception and Family Planning

Now, folks, we can't talk about sexual health without getting down and dirty with contraception and family planning. Get ready to plunge headfirst into the world of contraceptive methods. We'll explore everything from their effectiveness to how they're used and any potential side effects. Plus, we'll tackle the oh-so-important topic of family planning, giving you the lowdown on how to have those conversations with your partner and healthcare provider. By the end of this chapter, you'll have all the knowledge you need to make responsible choices about your reproductive health. You're about to become a master of your own destiny, my friends.

6: Safer Sex and STI Prevention

Listen up, everyone, because we're about to get real about sexually transmitted infections (STIs). No need to panic, though, because we've got your back. We're diving into the wonderful world of safer sex practices, revealing all the methods that can lower your chances of getting an STI. Condom usage, regular testing

- we're giving you the lowdown on it all. Armed with the latest evidence-based information, you'll be ready to protect yourself and your partner from any unpleasant consequences that come with unprotected encounters. It's time to stay safe and sizzle, my friends.

7: Healthy Body Image and Self-Acceptance

Hold onto your hats, folks, because we're about to float into the realm of body image and self-acceptance. It's time to break free from the chains that hold us back from loving ourselves. We're delving deep into the tangled web of body image, and trust me, it's a wild ride. By the time we're finished here, you'll be a master of media literacy, self-esteem building, and body positivity. Say goodbye to negative chatter in your mind and hello to a healthy perspective on beauty and self-worth. It's time to embrace your unique self and let your confidence soar.

8: LGBTQ+ Inclusivity

Oh, baby, inclusivity is the name of the game. In this chapter, we're paving the way for all our diverse and fabulous friends. It doesn't matter who you love or how you identify - we've got your back. We're diving into the challenges faced by LGBTQ+ individuals when it comes to accessing sexual health resources. And, my friends, we're here to bridge that gap. We'll give you the knowledge and support you need to navigate your sexual and gender identities with pride and confidence. It's time to celebrate love in all its beautiful forms.

Epilogue: A Future of Empowered Choices

Hold on tight, my friends, because we're coming to the end of this incredible journey. Take a moment to reflect on all the knowledge you've gained and the possibilities that lie ahead. We're here to celebrate you, to empower you to embrace your sexual well-being, and to make choices that truly align with your values, desires, and dreams. With a newfound sense of confidence, compassion, and understanding, you're equipped to conquer the complex terrain of sexual relationships. And guess what? You're not just equipped for your own journey, my friends - you're also equipped to spread the word and advocate for inclusive sexual health education in your communities. Together, we're unlocking a world of knowledge, empowerment, and endless possibilities. Join us on this extraordinary adventure - Test Treasure Publication is ready to light the way.

# 8.1 Full-Length Practice Test 1

## Section 1: Physical Education Content Knowledge

### Topic: Basics of Physical Education

**Question 1:** What is the primary purpose of Physical Education in schools?
A) Improve academic performance
B) Teach sportsmanship
C) Promote physical fitness
D) Develop social skills

### Topic: Motor Learning and Skills

**Question 2:** What type of motor skill is swimming?
A) Fine motor skill
B) Gross motor skill
C) Serial skill
D) Discrete skill

### Topic: Anatomy and Physiology in Physical Education

**Question 3:** Which muscle is primarily responsible for elbow flexion?

A) Quadriceps

B) Deltoid

C) Biceps

D) Triceps

**Topic: Sports Psychology**

**Question 4:** What is the term for anxiety felt before a competition?

A) Eustress

B) Flow

C) Burnout

D) Pre-competition anxiety

**Topic: Fitness Assessment and Evaluation**

**Question 5:** What is measured in the Beep Test?

A) Strength

B) Flexibility

C) Cardiovascular endurance

D) Balance

# Section 2: Student Growth and Development

**Topic: Childhood Development Theories**

**Question 6:** Whose theory focused on the psychological impact of social experiences across the whole lifespan?
A) Piaget
B) Erikson
C) Maslow
D) Vygotsky

## Topic: Physical Development Milestones

**Question 7:** At what age do children generally begin to walk unaided?
A) 6-9 months
B) 10-14 months
C) 15-18 months
D) 19-24 months

## Topic: Cognitive Development in Children

**Question 8:** According to Piaget, in which stage do children begin to think logically about concrete events?
A) Sensorimotor
B) Preoperational
C) Concrete operational
D) Formal operational

## Topic: Social and Emotional Development

**Question 9:** What is 'Attachment Theory' primarily concerned with?
A) Cognitive development

B) Social relationships

C) Emotional regulation

D) Language acquisition

## Section 3: Management, Motivation, and Communication

### Topic: Classroom Management Techniques

**Question 10:** Which technique is often used to manage students' behavior through a reward system?
A) Extrinsic motivation
B) Proximity control
C) Time-out
D) Withitness

### Topic: Motivational Strategies

**Question 11:** What is the motivational strategy that involves breaking long-term goals into smaller, achievable parts?
A) Scaffolding
B) Goal-setting
C) Self-efficacy
D) Self-determination

### Topic: Communication Skills for Teachers

**Question 12:** What type of questions require more than a 'yes' or 'no' answer?

A) Closed-ended questions

B) Open-ended questions

C) Leading questions

D) Rhetorical questions

**Topic: Conflict Resolution**

**Question 13:** Which conflict resolution strategy involves finding a solution that partially satisfies all parties involved?

A) Avoidance

B) Accommodation

C) Compromise

D) Collaboration

# Section 4: Planning, Instruction, and Student Assessment

**Topic: Curriculum Planning and Design**

**Question 14:** What is 'Backward Design'?

A) Starting with learning objectives and working backward to plan instruction

B) Introducing new concepts before revising old ones

C) Focusing only on assessment techniques

D) Preparing for only the first half of the curriculum

**Topic: Instructional Strategies**

**Question 15:** What is the instructional strategy that involves students teaching other students?

A) Direct instruction
B) Cooperative learning
C) Peer teaching
D) Inquiry-based learning

**Topic: Formative and Summative Assessments**

**Question 16:** Which type of assessment aims to monitor student learning to provide ongoing feedback?

A) Diagnostic assessment
B) Formative assessment
C) Summative assessment
D) Benchmark assessment

**Topic: Feedback Mechanisms**

**Question 17:** What is the purpose of 'Constructive Feedback'?

A) To punish the student
B) To provide information that will help improve performance
C) To compare a student to their peers
D) To finalize grades

## Section 5: Collaboration, Reflection, and Technology

**Topic: Teamwork and Collaboration in Education**

**Question 18:** What is a 'Professional Learning Community' (PLC)?

A) An online course for teachers

B) A group of educators committed to working collaboratively

C) A mandatory state training program for teachers

D) An educational conference

**Topic: Reflective Teaching Practices**

**Question 19:** What does the term 'Reflective Practice' involve?

A) Revising lesson plans only when necessary

B) Thinking critically about one's own teaching practice

C) Following standard teaching guidelines

D) Copying other successful teachers

**Topic: Technology Integration in Physical Education**

**Question 20:** What is the main advantage of using fitness tracking devices in Physical Education classes?

A) To replace the teacher

B) To provide real-time data on student performance

C) To entertain students

D) To complete administrative tasks

# Section 6: Health Education as a Discipline

**Topic: Introduction to Health Education**

**Question 21:** What is the primary focus of health education?

A) Physical fitness

B) Disease prevention

C) Nutrition

D) All of the above


**Topic: Health Promotion Theories**

**Question 22:** What theory emphasizes the influence of social factors on health behavior?

A) Health Belief Model

B) Social Cognitive Theory

C) Transtheoretical Model

D) Theory of Reasoned Action


**Topic: Ethics in Health Education**

**Question 23:** What is the principle that refers to doing no harm?

A) Autonomy

B) Beneficence

C) Non-maleficence

D) Justice


**Topic: Community and Public Health**

**Question 24:** What is the primary goal of community health education?

A) Increase healthcare profits

B) Promote individual well-being

C) Enhance public health

D) Address individual medical conditions

## Section 7: Health Education Content

### Topic: Nutrition and Healthy Eating Habits

**Question 25:** What nutrient is the main source of energy for the body?

A) Protein

B) Fat

C) Carbohydrates

D) Vitamins

### Topic: Physical Activity and Wellness

**Question 26:** What type of exercise is best for improving cardiovascular endurance?

A) Anaerobic exercise

B) Strength training

C) Aerobic exercise

D) Flexibility training

### Topic: Mental and Emotional Health

**Question 27:** What is Emotional Intelligence primarily concerned with?

A) IQ score

B) Understanding and managing one's emotions

C) Career success

D) Academic achievement

**Topic: Substance Abuse Education**

**Question 28:** What is the primary reason teenagers give for using drugs?

A) Curiosity

B) Peer pressure

C) Self-medication

D) All of the above

**Topic: Sexual Health Education**

**Question 29:** What is the most effective method for preventing pregnancy and sexually transmitted diseases?

A) Abstinence

B) Birth control pills

C) Condoms

D) Periodic abstinence

**Topic: Substance Abuse Education (Additional)**

**Question 30:** Which drug is classified as a depressant?

A) Cocaine

B) LSD

C) Alcohol

D) Caffeine

# Section 1: Physical Education Content Knowledge

## Topic: Basics of Physical Education

**Question 31:** What is the primary goal of physical education?
A) Weight loss
B) Skill development
C) Competitive sports
D) Academic improvement

## Topic: Motor Learning and Skills

**Question 32:** What does 'kinesthetic awareness' refer to?
A) Memory of movement
B) Sensation of movement
C) Speed of movement
D) Quality of movement

## Topic: Anatomy and Physiology in Physical Education

**Question 33:** What muscle is primarily used in push-ups?
A) Latissimus dorsi
B) Pectoralis major
C) Biceps
D) Triceps

**Topic: Sports Psychology**

**Question 34:** Which term describes an athlete's ability to maintain focus?
A) Attention span
B) Concentration
C) Awareness
D) Motivation

**Topic: Fitness Assessment and Evaluation**

**Question 35:** What is the Body Mass Index (BMI) used to assess?
A) Strength
B) Flexibility
C) Body composition
D) Cardiovascular fitness

# Section 2: Student Growth and Development

## Topic: Childhood Development Theories

**Question 36:** Who proposed the theory of 'Psychosocial Development'?
A) Erik Erikson
B) Sigmund Freud
C) Jean Piaget
D) Lev Vygotsky

## Topic: Physical Development Milestones

**Question 37:** At what age do most children learn to walk independently?
A) 6-9 months
B) 10-14 months
C) 15-18 months
D) 19-24 months

**Topic: Cognitive Development in Children**

**Question 38:** During which stage of cognitive development do children begin to use logic according to Piaget?
A) Sensorimotor
B) Preoperational
C) Concrete operational
D) Formal operational

**Topic: Social and Emotional Development**

**Question 39:** What type of play involves children playing side-by-side but not with each other?
A) Solitary play
B) Parallel play
C) Associative play
D) Cooperative play

# Section 3: Management, Motivation, and Communication

**Topic: Classroom Management Techniques**

**Question 40:** Which classroom management technique involves giving students choices?

A) Authoritative strategy

B) Behavioral modification

C) Choice theory

D) Time-out

## Topic: Motivational Strategies

**Question 41:** Which motivational theory focuses on intrinsic and extrinsic motivators?

A) Maslow's Hierarchy of Needs

B) Expectancy Theory

C) Self-Determination Theory

D) Herzberg's Two-Factor Theory

## Topic: Communication Skills for Teachers

**Question 42:** What is an example of non-verbal communication?

A) Writing

B) Gesturing

C) Speaking

D) Listening

## Topic: Conflict Resolution

**Question 43:** Which conflict resolution strategy involves finding a middle ground?

A) Accommodating
B) Avoiding
C) Compromising
D) Collaborating

## Section 4: Planning, Instruction, and Student Assessment

### Topic: Curriculum Planning and Design

**Question 44:** What is 'backward design'?
A) Planning instruction based on desired outcomes
B) Planning instruction based on available resources
C) Planning instruction starting from the most complex tasks
D) Planning instruction based on students' prior knowledge

### Topic: Instructional Strategies

**Question 45:** What type of learning involves hands-on activities?
A) Auditory learning
B) Visual learning
C) Kinesthetic learning
D) Read/write learning

### Topic: Formative and Summative Assessments

**Question 46:** Which type of assessment is typically graded?
A) Formative assessment

B) Summative assessment
C) Diagnostic assessment
D) Informal assessment

**Topic: Feedback Mechanisms**

**Question 47:** What type of feedback focuses on the process rather than the end result?
A) Corrective feedback
B) Outcome feedback
C) Process feedback
D) Positive feedback

# Section 5: Collaboration, Reflection, and Technology

**Topic: Teamwork and Collaboration in Education**

**Question 48:** What is the primary benefit of collaborative learning?
A) Increases teacher control
B) Increases individual performance
C) Develops social skills
D) Reduces workload for the teacher

**Topic: Reflective Teaching Practices**

**Question 49:** What is the ultimate aim of reflective teaching?
A) Reduced planning

B) Improved instruction

C) Easier classroom management

D) Higher test scores

**Topic: Technology Integration in Physical Education**

**Question 50:** What technology can be used to monitor students' heart rates during physical activities?

A) Interactive whiteboards

B) Virtual reality

C) Heart rate monitors

D) Tablet computers

## Section 6: Health Education as a Discipline

**Topic: Introduction to Health Education**

**Question 51:** What is the primary focus of health education?

A) Disease prevention

B) Treatment of illness

C) Physical fitness

D) Mental wellness

**Topic: Health Promotion Theories**

**Question 52:** Which theory emphasizes the influence of social factors on health behavior?

A) Health Belief Model

B) Social Cognitive Theory

C) Theory of Planned Behavior

D) Transtheoretical Model

**Topic: Ethics in Health Education**

**Question 53:** What is the primary ethical principle in health education?

A) Autonomy

B) Non-maleficence

C) Beneficence

D) Justice

**Topic: Community and Public Health**

**Question 54:** What approach focuses on the health of the entire community?

A) Clinical approach

B) Epidemiological approach

C) Public health approach

D) Therapeutic approach

## Section 7: Health Education Content

**Topic: Nutrition and Healthy Eating Habits**

**Question 55:** Which vitamin is primarily responsible for bone health?

A) Vitamin A

B) Vitamin C
C) Vitamin D
D) Vitamin E

**Topic: Physical Activity and Wellness**

**Question 56:** What is the recommended amount of physical activity for adults per week according to the CDC?
A) 75 minutes
B) 150 minutes
C) 200 minutes
D) 300 minutes

**Topic: Mental and Emotional Health**

**Question 57:** What is the primary hormone associated with stress?
A) Insulin
B) Adrenaline
C) Cortisol
D) Serotonin

**Topic: Substance Abuse Education**

**Question 58:** Which is a common sign of alcohol abuse?
A) Increased sociability
B) Improved focus
C) Decreased inhibitions
D) Improved motor skills

**Topic: Sexual Health Education**

**Question 59:** What is the primary method for preventing STIs during sexual activity?
A) Birth control pills
B) Abstinence
C) Vaccination
D) Barrier methods

**Question 60:** Which nutrient is most important for muscle repair and growth?
A) Carbohydrates
B) Proteins
C) Fats
D) Vitamins

# Section 1: Physical Education Content Knowledge

**Topic: Basics of Physical Education**

**Question 61:** What is the primary aim of Physical Education?
A) Competition
B) Skill Acquisition
C) Physical Fitness
D) Social Interaction

## Topic: Motor Learning and Skills

**Question 62:** What does "kinesthesia" refer to?
A) Muscular strength
B) Body awareness
C) Flexibility
D) Reaction time

## Topic: Anatomy and Physiology in Physical Education

**Question 63:** Which system controls voluntary muscle movements?
A) Nervous System
B) Muscular System
C) Skeletal System
D) Endocrine System

## Topic: Sports Psychology

**Question 64:** What is the term for fear of failure in sports?
A) Anxiety
B) Stress
C) Atelophobia
D) Apathy

## Topic: Fitness Assessment and Evaluation

**Question 65:** Which test measures cardiovascular endurance?
A) Sit and Reach

B) One-rep max
C) Body Mass Index
D) Cooper Test

## Section 2: Student Growth and Development

### Topic: Childhood Development Theories

**Question 66:** Who proposed the theory of "Zone of Proximal Development"?
A) Erik Erikson
B) Jean Piaget
C) Sigmund Freud
D) Lev Vygotsky

### Topic: Physical Development Milestones

**Question 67:** At what age do most children start walking?
A) 6-9 months
B) 9-12 months
C) 12-18 months
D) 18-24 months

### Topic: Cognitive Development in Children

**Question 68:** Which cognitive stage occurs from age 2 to 7, according to Piaget?
A) Sensorimotor
B) Preoperational

C) Concrete operational
D) Formal operational

**Topic: Social and Emotional Development**

**Question 69:** What is the primary focus during Erikson's "Industry vs. Inferiority" stage?
A) Trust
B) Autonomy
C) Competence
D) Identity

## Section 3: Management, Motivation, and Communication

**Topic: Classroom Management Techniques**

**Question 70:** What is the primary purpose of a classroom contract?
A) To establish rules
B) To define punishments
C) To improve academic performance
D) To establish teacher authority

**Topic: Motivational Strategies**

**Question 71:** What type of motivation comes from external rewards?
A) Intrinsic motivation
B) Extrinsic motivation

C) Amotivation
D) None of the above

**Topic: Communication Skills for Teachers**

**Question 72:** What is active listening?
A) Interpreting the message while listening
B) Providing feedback while listening
C) Both A and B
D) Neither A nor B

**Topic: Conflict Resolution**

**Question 73:** Which conflict resolution strategy involves both parties giving up something?
A) Avoiding
B) Accommodating
C) Compromising
D) Collaborating

# Section 4: Planning, Instruction, and Student Assessment

**Topic: Curriculum Planning and Design**

**Question 74:** What is the most flexible type of curriculum design?
A) Subject-Centered
B) Learner-Centered

C) Problem-Centered
D) Standardized

## Topic: Instructional Strategies

**Question 75:** What teaching strategy uses a problem-solving approach to enable student discovery?
A) Lecture method
B) Inquiry-based learning
C) Role-playing
D) Demonstration

## Topic: Formative and Summative Assessments

**Question 76:** Which assessment is usually conducted at the end of a course?
A) Diagnostic
B) Formative
C) Summative
D) Continuous

## Topic: Feedback Mechanisms

**Question 77:** What type of feedback focuses on the task rather than the student?
A) Positive Feedback
B) Negative Feedback
C) Task-Oriented Feedback
D) Ego-Oriented Feedback

# Section 5: Collaboration, Reflection, and Technology

## Topic: Teamwork and Collaboration in Education

**Question 78:** What is the primary purpose of cooperative learning?
A) Individual accountability
B) Socialization
C) Academic achievement
D) Both A and C


## Topic: Reflective Teaching Practices

**Question 79:** What is the purpose of a teaching portfolio?
A) Assessment
B) Reflection
C) Professional Development
D) All of the above


## Topic: Technology Integration in Physical Education

**Question 80:** What technology is most commonly used to track physical performance in real-time?
A) Smartboards
B) Projectors
C) Wearable fitness trackers
D) Virtual Reality

## Section 6: Health Education as a Discipline

### Topic: Introduction to Health Education

**Question 81:** What is the primary aim of health education?
A) Prevention of diseases
B) Promotion of health
C) Both A and B
D) None of the above

### Topic: Health Promotion Theories

**Question 82:** Which theory focuses on the perceived benefits vs. perceived barriers to taking action?
A) Social Cognitive Theory
B) Health Belief Model
C) Transtheoretical Model
D) Theory of Planned Behavior

### Topic: Ethics in Health Education

**Question 83:** Which ethical principle emphasizes doing no harm?
A) Autonomy
B) Beneficence
C) Non-maleficence
D) Justice

### Topic: Community and Public Health

**Question 84:** What is epidemiology primarily concerned with?

A) Treatment of diseases

B) Prevention of diseases

C) Study of diseases distribution

D) Cure of diseases

## Section 7: Health Education Content

### Topic: Nutrition and Healthy Eating Habits

**Question 85:** What nutrient provides the most energy per gram?

A) Protein

B) Carbohydrates

C) Fats

D) Vitamins

### Topic: Physical Activity and Wellness

**Question 86:** What is the recommended amount of moderate exercise per week for adults?

A) 75 minutes

B) 150 minutes

C) 200 minutes

D) 300 minutes

## Topic: Mental and Emotional Health

**Question 87:** Which hormone is known as the "stress hormone"?

A) Adrenaline

B) Cortisol

C) Dopamine

D) Serotonin

## Topic: Substance Abuse Education

**Question 88:** What is the legal blood alcohol concentration (BAC) limit for driving in most U.S. states?

A) 0.05%

B) 0.08%

C) 0.10%

D) 0.12%

## Topic: Sexual Health Education

**Question 89:** What is the most effective method of birth control, besides abstinence?

A) Condoms

B) Birth Control Pills

C) Intrauterine Device (IUD)

D) Diaphragm

## Section 1: Physical Education Content Knowledge

### Topic: Fitness Assessment and Evaluation

**Question 90:** What does the Body Mass Index (BMI) primarily measure?
A) Cardiovascular fitness
B) Muscular strength
C) Body composition
D) Flexibility

## Section 2: Student Growth and Development

### Topic: Social and Emotional Development

**Question 91:** Which theory suggests that emotional intelligence is just as important as traditional IQ for success?
A) Gardner's Multiple Intelligences
B) Freud's Psychosexual Stages
C) Erikson's Psychosocial Stages
D) Goleman's Emotional Intelligence

## Section 3: Management, Motivation, and Communication

### Topic: Communication Skills for Teachers

**Question 92:** Which communication style is generally most effective in a classroom setting?
A) Passive

B) Aggressive

C) Assertive

D) Passive-Aggressive

## Section 4: Planning, Instruction, and Student Assessment

### Topic: Curriculum Planning and Design

**Question 93:** Which educational approach integrates subjects across the curriculum?

A) Traditional

B) Interdisciplinary

C) Skill-based

D) Student-centered

## Section 5: Collaboration, Reflection, and Technology

### Topic: Professional Development Resources

**Question 94:** What is the primary purpose of Professional Learning Communities (PLC)?

A) Networking

B) Collaboration

C) Skill improvement

D) Both B and C

## Section 6: Health Education as a Discipline

### Topic: Community and Public Health

**Question 95:** What is the primary goal of public health?
A) Disease treatment
B) Disease prevention
C) Medical research
D) Health advocacy

## Section 7: Health Education Content

### Topic: Substance Abuse Education

**Question 96:** What is the most commonly abused illegal drug in the U.S.?
A) Cocaine
B) Heroin
C) Marijuana
D) Methamphetamine

## Section 1: Physical Education Content Knowledge (Extra Topic)

### Topic: Motor Learning and Skills

**Question 97:** What type of motor skill is riding a bicycle?
A) Gross motor skill
B) Fine motor skill

C) Both A and B
D) Neither A nor B

## Section 2: Student Growth and Development (Extra Topic)

### Topic: Cognitive Development in Children

**Question 98:** Who proposed the Zone of Proximal Development (ZPD)?
A) Jean Piaget
B) Erik Erikson
C) Lev Vygotsky
D) John Bowlby

## Section 3: Management, Motivation, and Communication (Extra Topic)

### Topic: Conflict Resolution

**Question 99:** What is the first step in conflict resolution?
A) Seeking a compromise
B) Identifying the problem
C) Implementing a solution
D) Avoiding the conflict

## Section 4: Planning, Instruction, and Student Assessment (Extra Topic)

**Topic: Feedback Mechanisms**

**Question 100:** What type of feedback is immediate and comes during the learning process?
A) Summative
B) Formative
C) Delayed
D) None of the above

# 8.2 Answer Sheet – Practice Test 1

**1. Answer:** C) Promote physical fitness

**Explanation:** The primary goal of Physical Education in schools is to promote physical fitness and teach students the importance of maintaining a healthy lifestyle.

**2. Answer:** B) Gross motor skill

**Explanation:** Swimming involves large muscle groups and coordinated movement, making it a gross motor skill.

**3. Answer:** C) Biceps

**Explanation:** The biceps muscle is responsible for flexing the elbow joint.

**4. Answer:** D) Pre-competition anxiety

**Explanation:** Anxiety experienced specifically before a competition is known as pre-competition anxiety.

**5. Answer:** C) Cardiovascular endurance

**Explanation:** The Beep Test measures cardiovascular endurance by requiring participants to run back and forth between markers at increasing speeds.

**6. Answer:** B) Erikson

**Explanation:** Erik Erikson's theory of psychosocial development focuses on the impact of social experiences throughout the lifespan.

**7. Answer:** B) 10-14 months

**Explanation:** Most children start to walk unaided between 10 to 14 months of age.

**8. Answer:** C) Concrete operational

**Explanation:** In Piaget's theory, the Concrete Operational stage (ages 7-11) is when children begin to think logically about concrete events.

**9. Answer:** B) Social relationships

**Explanation:** Attachment Theory primarily focuses on the importance of social relationships, especially the bonds between children and their caregivers.

**10. Answer:** A) Extrinsic motivation

**Explanation:** Extrinsic motivation often involves the use of rewards to influence student behavior positively.

**11. Answer:** B) Goal-setting

**Explanation:** Goal-setting involves breaking down long-term goals into smaller, more manageable parts to make them achievable and motivate individuals.

**12. Answer:** B) Open-ended questions

**Explanation:** Open-ended questions require more than a simple 'yes' or 'no' answer and encourage discussion.

**13. Answer:** C) Compromise

**Explanation:** Compromise involves finding a middle ground where all parties can be partially satisfied.

**14. Answer:** A) Starting with learning objectives and working backward to plan instruction

**Explanation:** Backward Design starts with the end goals or learning objectives and then plans instructional methods and assessments that will help students achieve those goals.

**15. Answer:** C) Peer teaching

**Explanation:** Peer teaching is an instructional strategy where students are responsible for teaching their peers.

**16. Answer:** B) Formative assessment

**Explanation:** Formative assessment is used to provide continuous feedback and adjust instructional methods to improve student learning.

**17. Answer:** B) To provide information that will help improve performance

**Explanation:** The primary purpose of Constructive Feedback is to offer valuable information that helps improve future performance.

**18. Answer:** B) A group of educators committed to working collaboratively

**Explanation:** A Professional Learning Community (PLC) is a group of educators who work together to improve teaching skills and the academic performance of students.

**19. Answer:** B) Thinking critically about one's own teaching practice

**Explanation:** Reflective Practice involves ongoing critical thinking about one's teaching methods and adjustments based on those reflections.

**20. Answer:** B) To provide real-time data on student performance

**Explanation:** Fitness tracking devices provide real-time data that can help both the teacher and students understand performance levels and make necessary adjustments.

**21. Answer:** D) All of the above

**Explanation:** Health education focuses on a variety of topics, including physical fitness, disease prevention, and nutrition, to promote overall well-being.

**22. Answer:** B) Social Cognitive Theory

**Explanation:** Social Cognitive Theory emphasizes the role of social factors, observational learning, and interactions in shaping health behavior.

**23. Answer:** C) Non-maleficence

**Explanation:** Non-maleficence refers to the ethical principle of doing no harm.

**24. Answer:** C) Enhance public health

**Explanation:** The primary goal of community health education is to enhance the overall health of the community.

**25. Answer:** C) Carbohydrates

**Explanation:** Carbohydrates are the body's primary source of energy.

**26. Answer:** C) Aerobic exercise

**Explanation:** Aerobic exercise, such as running or swimming, is best for improving cardiovascular endurance.

**27. Answer:** B) Understanding and managing one's emotions

**Explanation:** Emotional Intelligence is primarily concerned with the ability to understand and manage one's emotions, as well as the emotions of others.

**28. Answer:** B) Peer pressure

**Explanation:** Peer pressure is often cited as the primary reason teenagers begin to use drugs.

**29. Answer:** A) Abstinence

**Explanation:** Abstinence from sexual activity is the only method that is 100% effective in preventing both pregnancy and sexually transmitted diseases.

**30. Answer:** C) Alcohol

**Explanation:** Alcohol is classified as a depressant because it slows down the central nervous system.

**31. Answer:** B) Skill development

**Explanation:** The primary goal of physical education is skill development and cultivating a lifelong interest in physical activity.

**32. Answer:** B) Sensation of movement

**Explanation:** Kinesthetic awareness refers to the sensation of movement and position of body parts.

**33. Answer:** B) Pectoralis major

**Explanation:** The pectoralis major muscle is primarily used during push-ups.

**34. Answer:** B) Concentration

**Explanation:** Concentration refers to an athlete's ability to maintain focus over a period of time.

**35. Answer:** C) Body composition

**Explanation:** BMI is used to provide a quick assessment of body composition.

**36. Answer:** A) Erik Erikson

**Explanation:** Erik Erikson is known for his theory of 'Psychosocial Development.'

**37. Answer:** B) 10-14 months

**Explanation:** Most children begin to walk independently between 10 to 14 months.

**38. Answer:** C) Concrete operational

**Explanation:** According to Piaget, children begin to use logic during the 'Concrete Operational' stage.

**39. Answer:** B) Parallel play

**Explanation:** Parallel play involves children playing side-by-side but not directly interacting with each other.

**40. Answer:** C) Choice theory

**Explanation:** Choice theory emphasizes empowering students by giving them choices.

**41. Answer:** C) Self-Determination Theory

**Explanation:** Self-Determination Theory focuses on the interplay between intrinsic and extrinsic motivators.

**42. Answer:** B) Gesturing

**Explanation:** Gesturing is an example of non-verbal communication.

**43. Answer:** C) Compromising

**Explanation:** Compromising as a conflict resolution strategy involves finding a middle ground where both parties give something up to resolve the conflict.

**44. Answer:** A) Planning instruction based on desired outcomes

**Explanation:** 'Backward design' starts with the end goals and plans instruction to achieve those outcomes.

**45. Answer:** C) Kinesthetic learning

**Explanation:** Kinesthetic learning involves physical activities or hands-on tasks.

**46. Answer:** B) Summative assessment

**Explanation:** Summative assessments are typically graded and occur at the end of an instructional period.

**47. Answer:** C) Process feedback

**Explanation:** Process feedback focuses on the tasks and activities leading to the end result.

**48. Answer:** C) Develops social skills

**Explanation:** Collaborative learning primarily helps in the development of social skills among students.

**49. Answer:** B) Improved instruction

**Explanation:** The ultimate aim of reflective teaching is to improve instruction and enhance learning.

**50. Answer:** C) Heart rate monitors

**Explanation:** Heart rate monitors can be used to track students' physical exertion levels during activities.

**51. Answer:** A) Disease prevention

**Explanation:** The primary focus of health education is disease prevention and promoting healthy behaviors.

**52. Answer:** B) Social Cognitive Theory

**Explanation:** Social Cognitive Theory focuses on the impact of social factors on individual health behavior.

**53. Answer:** A) Autonomy

**Explanation:** Autonomy, or respect for individual choice, is considered the primary ethical principle in health education.

**54. Answer:** C) Public health approach

**Explanation:** The public health approach focuses on improving the health of the entire community.

**55. Answer:** C) Vitamin D

**Explanation:** Vitamin D plays a crucial role in calcium absorption, which is vital for bone health.

**56. Answer:** B) 150 minutes

**Explanation:** According to the CDC, adults should aim for at least 150 minutes of moderate-intensity aerobic activity every week.

**57. Answer:** C) Cortisol

**Explanation:** Cortisol is the primary hormone released during stress.

**58. Answer:** C) Decreased inhibitions

**Explanation:** A common sign of alcohol abuse is decreased inhibitions, leading to risky behaviors.

**59. Answer:** D) Barrier methods

**Explanation:** Barrier methods like condoms are the primary method for preventing the spread of STIs during sexual activity.

**60. Answer:** B) Proteins

**Explanation:** Proteins are essential for muscle repair and growth, as they provide the building blocks for muscle tissues.

**61. Answer:** C) Physical Fitness

**Explanation:** The primary aim of Physical Education is to improve physical fitness and overall well-being.

**62. Answer:** B) Body awareness

**Explanation:** Kinesthesia refers to the sense of body position and movement.

**63. Answer:** A) Nervous System

**Explanation:** The nervous system controls voluntary muscle movements.

**64. Answer:** C) Atelophobia

**Explanation:** Atelophobia is the fear of not being good enough, or fear of failure.

**65. Answer:** D) Cooper Test

**Explanation:** The Cooper Test is used to measure cardiovascular endurance.

**66. Answer:** D) Lev Vygotsky

**Explanation:** Lev Vygotsky proposed the theory of the Zone of Proximal Development.

**67. Answer:** C) 12-18 months

**Explanation:** Most children start walking between 12 and 18 months.

**68. Answer:** B) Preoperational

**Explanation:** According to Piaget, the preoperational stage occurs from age 2 to 7.

**69. Answer:** C) Competence

**Explanation:** The primary focus during this stage is on developing competence.

**70. Answer:** A) To establish rules

**Explanation:** A classroom contract primarily aims to establish classroom rules that students agree to follow.

**71. Answer:** B) Extrinsic motivation

**Explanation:** Extrinsic motivation comes from external factors like rewards and punishments.

**72. Answer:** C) Both A and B

**Explanation:** Active listening involves interpreting the message and providing feedback while listening.

**73. Answer:** C) Compromising

**Explanation:** Compromising involves both parties giving up something to resolve the conflict.

**74. Answer:** B) Learner-Centered

**Explanation:** A learner-centered curriculum is the most flexible as it is tailored to the needs and interests of the students.

**75. Answer:** B) Inquiry-based learning

**Explanation:** Inquiry-based learning uses a problem-solving approach to encourage student discovery.

**76. Answer:** C) Summative

**Explanation:** Summative assessments are typically conducted at the end of a course to evaluate overall learning.

**77. Answer:** C) Task-Oriented Feedback

**Explanation:** Task-oriented feedback focuses on the task and how it can be improved, rather than focusing on the student.

**78. Answer:** D) Both A and C

**Explanation:** The primary purpose of cooperative learning is both individual accountability and academic achievement.

**79. Answer:** D) All of the above

**Explanation:** A teaching portfolio serves for assessment, reflection, and professional development.

**80. Answer:** C) Wearable fitness trackers

**Explanation:** Wearable fitness trackers are commonly used to track physical performance in real-time.

**81. Answer:** C) Both A and B

**Explanation:** The primary aim of health education is both prevention of diseases and promotion of health.

**82. Answer:** B) Health Belief Model

**Explanation:** The Health Belief Model focuses on perceived benefits versus perceived barriers to taking action.

**83. Answer:** C) Non-maleficence

**Explanation:** The principle of non-maleficence emphasizes doing no harm.

**84. Answer:** C) Study of diseases distribution

**Explanation:** Epidemiology is primarily concerned with the study of the distribution and determinants of diseases in populations.

**85. Answer:** C) Fats

**Explanation:** Fats provide the most energy per gram, at 9 calories per gram.

**86. Answer:** B) 150 minutes

**Explanation:** The recommended amount of moderate exercise for adults is 150 minutes per week.

**87. Answer:** B) Cortisol

**Explanation:** Cortisol is commonly referred to as the "stress hormone."

**88. Answer:** B) 0.08%

**Explanation:** The legal BAC limit for driving in most U.S. states is 0.08%.

**89. Answer:** C) Intrauterine Device (IUD)

**Explanation:** The IUD is the most effective method of birth control, besides abstinence.

**90. Answer:** C) Body composition

**Explanation:** BMI primarily measures body composition, which is an indicator of body fat in relation to height and weight.

**91. Answer:** D) Goleman's Emotional Intelligence

**Explanation:** Daniel Goleman's theory of Emotional Intelligence argues that EQ is as important as IQ for success.

**92. Answer:** C) Assertive

**Explanation:** Assertive communication is generally the most effective style for a classroom setting, as it promotes clarity and mutual respect.

**93. Answer:** B) Interdisciplinary

**Explanation:** An interdisciplinary approach integrates subjects across the curriculum to provide a more holistic education.

**94. Answer:** D) Both B and C

**Explanation:** The primary purpose of PLCs is both for collaboration among educators and skill improvement.

**95. Answer:** B) Disease prevention

**Explanation:** The primary goal of public health is disease prevention to improve community health.

**96. Answer:** C) Marijuana

**Explanation:** Marijuana is the most commonly abused illegal drug in the United States.

**97. Answer:** A) Gross motor skill

**Explanation:** Riding a bicycle is a gross motor skill, as it requires the use of large muscle groups for balance and coordination.

**98. Answer:** C) Lev Vygotsky

**Explanation:** Lev Vygotsky proposed the Zone of Proximal Development, which is the difference between what a learner can do without help and what they can do with guidance.

**99. Answer:** B) Identifying the problem

**Explanation:** The first step in conflict resolution is identifying the problem or the source of the conflict.

**100. Answer:** B) Formative

**Explanation:** Formative feedback is immediate and occurs during the learning process to improve performance.

# 9.1 Full-Length Practice Test 2

## Section 1: Physical Education Content Knowledge

### Topic: Basics of Physical Education

**Question 101:** What is the primary objective of physical education?
A) Athletic performance
B) Socialization
C) Physical fitness
D) Academic improvement

### Topic: Motor Learning and Skills

**Question 102:** What is a closed skill in motor learning?
A) Skills performed in a changing environment
B) Skills performed in a predictable environment
C) Skills requiring team coordination
D) Skills requiring quick reflexes

### Topic: Anatomy and Physiology in Physical Education

**Question 103:** Which muscle type is responsible for the movement of the digestive system?
A) Skeletal
B) Smooth
C) Cardiac
D) None of the above

### Topic: Sports Psychology

**Question 104:** Which psychological theory focuses on the role of reinforcement in motivation?
A) Maslow's Hierarchy of Needs
B) Operant Conditioning
C) Self-Determination Theory
D) Flow Theory

### Topic: Fitness Assessment and Evaluation

**Question 105:** Which of the following is a field test for assessing cardiovascular fitness?
A) 1.5-mile run
B) Push-up test
C) Sit and reach
D) Body Mass Index (BMI)

## Section 2: Student Growth and Development

**Topic: Childhood Development Theories**

**Question 106:** Who proposed the theory of cognitive development that includes stages such as the sensorimotor and preoperational stages?
A) Erikson
B) Maslow
C) Vygotsky
D) Piaget

**Topic: Physical Development Milestones**

**Question 107:** At what age do most children typically begin to walk?
A) 6-9 months
B) 9-12 months
C) 12-15 months
D) 15-18 months

**Topic: Cognitive Development in Children**

**Question 108:** In Piaget's theory, during which stage do children begin to think logically about concrete events?
A) Sensorimotor
B) Preoperational
C) Concrete Operational
D) Formal Operational

**Topic: Social and Emotional Development**

**Question 109:** What is emotional regulation?
A) Ability to perform tasks
B) Ability to manage emotions
C) Ability to understand others' emotions
D) Ability to solve problems

# Section 3: Management, Motivation, and Communication

## Topic: Classroom Management Techniques

**Question 110:** What is a token economy system?
A) Students earn grades for participation
B) Students earn tokens for good behavior
C) Students are given free time as a reward
D) Students negotiate classroom rules

## Topic: Motivational Strategies

**Question 111:** What is intrinsic motivation?
A) Motivation from external rewards
B) Motivation from internal rewards
C) Motivation from peer pressure
D) Motivation from fear of punishment

## Topic: Communication Skills for Teachers

**Question 112:** What is active listening?
A) Interrupting the speaker to ask questions
B) Listening without making eye contact
C) Listening with full attention and providing feedback
D) Listening while doing other tasks

**Topic: Conflict Resolution**

**Question 113:** Which of the following is a collaborative conflict resolution style?
A) Avoiding
B) Competing
C) Compromising
D) Collaborating

# Section 4: Planning, Instruction, and Student Assessment

**Topic: Curriculum Planning and Design**

**Question 114:** What is a spiral curriculum?
A) A curriculum that focuses only on core subjects
B) A curriculum that revisits topics at increasing levels of difficulty
C) A curriculum that follows a linear progression
D) A curriculum that allows students to choose subjects

**Topic: Instructional Strategies**

**Question 115:** What is the Socratic method?

A) Lecturing

B) Group discussions

C) Question and answer dialogue

D) Independent study

**Topic: Formative and Summative Assessments**

**Question 116:** Which is an example of a formative assessment?

A) Final exam

B) Quiz

C) Research paper

D) Presentation

**Topic: Feedback Mechanisms**

**Question 117:** What is constructive feedback?

A) Feedback that solely praises the student

B) Feedback that is overly critical

C) Feedback that helps improve performance

D) Feedback that compares one student to another

# Section 5: Collaboration, Reflection, and Technology

**Topic: Teamwork and Collaboration in Education**

**Question 118:** What is collaborative learning?

A) Independent study sessions

B) Learning through lectures

C) Learning in small groups

D) Learning through online courses

**Topic: Reflective Teaching Practices**

**Question 119:** What is a teaching portfolio used for?

A) To collect student work

B) To showcase a teacher's best practices

C) To gather textbooks and resources

D) To file administrative paperwork

**Topic: Technology Integration in Physical Education**

**Question 120:** Which technology can be used to analyze a student's running form in real-time?

A) Virtual reality

B) Biometric sensors

C) Video conferencing

D) Graphing calculators

**Topic: Professional Development Resources**

**Question 121:** What is the primary purpose of attending professional development workshops for teachers?

A) To meet state licensure requirements

B) To socialize with other teachers

C) To improve teaching skills and strategies

D) To secure promotions

## Section 6: Health Education as a Discipline

### Topic: Introduction to Health Education

**Question 122:** What is the primary focus of health education?

A) Physical fitness

B) Disease prevention

C) Emotional well-being

D) All of the above

### Topic: Health Promotion Theories

**Question 123:** What does the Health Belief Model focus on?

A) The role of healthcare systems

B) The role of individual beliefs in health behavior

C) The role of communities in health

D) The role of healthcare providers

### Topic: Ethics in Health Education

**Question 124:** What is informed consent in the context of health education?

A) Confidentiality agreements

B) Parental consent for minors

C) Understanding and agreeing to participate

D) None of the above

## Topic: Community and Public Health

**Question 125:** What is epidemiology?

A) Study of health education methods

B) Study of diseases and how they spread

C) Study of healthcare systems

D) Study of health and wellness programs

# Section 7: Health Education Content

## Topic: Nutrition and Healthy Eating Habits

**Question 126:** What does the term "caloric density" refer to?

A) Number of nutrients per serving

B) Number of calories per serving

C) Number of calories per gram of food

D) Nutrient absorption rate

## Topic: Physical Activity and Wellness

**Question 127:** What is the recommended amount of moderate exercise per week for adults?

A) 75 minutes

B) 150 minutes

C) 200 minutes
D) 300 minutes

**Topic: Mental and Emotional Health**

**Question 128:** What is mindfulness?
A) Focus on future goals
B) Awareness of present moment
C) Quick emotional responses
D) Multitasking efficiently

**Topic: Substance Abuse Education**

**Question 129:** What is the primary purpose of substance abuse education?
A) To punish users
B) To provide treatment
C) To prevent misuse
D) To provide legal information

**Topic: Sexual Health Education**

**Question 130:** What is the most effective method of preventing sexually transmitted infections (STIs)?
A) Abstinence
B) Vaccination
C) Condom use
D) Regular check-ups

# Section 1: Physical Education Content Knowledge

## Topic: Basics of Physical Education

**Question 131:** What is the primary goal of physical education?

A) Athletic competition

B) Physical fitness

C) Social interaction

D) Skill development

## Topic: Motor Learning and Skills

**Question 132:** What does the term "kinesthetic awareness" refer to?

A) Muscle strength

B) Awareness of body position

C) Cognitive understanding of movement

D) Respiratory efficiency

## Topic: Anatomy and Physiology in Physical Education

**Question 133:** What muscle type is the heart mainly composed of?

A) Smooth muscle

B) Skeletal muscle

C) Cardiac muscle

D) None of the above

## Topic: Sports Psychology

**Question 134:** What is "flow state" in sports psychology?

A) Distraction

B) Peak performance state

C) Anxiety

D) Lack of motivation

## Topic: Fitness Assessment and Evaluation

**Question 135:** What does VO2 max measure?

A) Strength

B) Speed

C) Aerobic capacity

D) Flexibility

# Section 2: Student Growth and Development

## Topic: Childhood Development Theories

**Question 136:** Who proposed the theory of psychosocial development?

A) Piaget

B) Maslow

C) Erikson

D) Skinner

## Topic: Physical Development Milestones

**Question 137:** At what age do children generally start walking?
A) 6-9 months
B) 10-14 months
C) 15-18 months
D) 19-24 months

**Topic: Cognitive Development in Children**

**Question 138:** What is "object permanence"?
A) Ability to sort objects
B) Understanding that objects exist even when not seen
C) Ability to identify colors
D) Understanding of spatial relationships

**Topic: Social and Emotional Development**

**Question 139:** What is "empathy"?
A) Social skills
B) Cognitive understanding
C) Understanding and sharing another person's feelings
D) Emotional intelligence

# Section 3: Management, Motivation, and Communication

**Topic: Classroom Management Techniques**

**Question 140:** What is the main goal of a classroom management plan?
A) To enforce discipline
B) To facilitate learning
C) To organize classroom activities
D) To comply with school policies

## Section 3: Management, Motivation, and Communication

### Topic: Motivational Strategies

**Question 141:** Which of the following is a type of extrinsic motivation?
A) Personal satisfaction
B) Trophy
C) Curiosity
D) Love for the activity

### Topic: Communication Skills for Teachers

**Question 142:** Which communication model involves a sender, message, and receiver?
A) Circular model
B) Linear model
C) Interactive model
D) All of the above

### Topic: Conflict Resolution

**Question 143:** What does the acronym "I-Messages" stand for in conflict resolution?
A) Issue
B) Intent
C) Information
D) Identification

# Section 4: Planning, Instruction, and Student Assessment

## Topic: Curriculum Planning and Design

**Question 144:** Which is NOT a type of curriculum design?
A) Subject-Centered
B) Learner-Centered
C) Problem-Centered
D) Community-Centered

## Topic: Instructional Strategies

**Question 145:** What is "scaffolding" in instructional strategies?
A) Evaluation process
B) Support mechanism to aid learning
C) Learning management system
D) Grouping students based on ability

## Topic: Formative and Summative Assessments

**Question 146:** Which assessment is conducted during the learning process?
A) Formative
B) Summative
C) Norm-referenced
D) Criterion-referenced

**Topic: Feedback Mechanisms**

**Question 147:** Which type of feedback focuses on the task rather than the learner?
A) Positive feedback
B) Negative feedback
C) Task-specific feedback
D) Personal feedback

## Section 5: Collaboration, Reflection, and Technology

### Topic: Teamwork and Collaboration in Education

**Question 148:** What is a "Professional Learning Community" (PLC)?
A) Online learning platform
B) Group of educators committed to working collaboratively
C) Government body regulating education
D) Collection of educational resources

### Topic: Reflective Teaching Practices

**Question 149:** What is the primary purpose of reflective teaching?

A) Compliance with school policies

B) Self-assessment and improvement

C) Peer evaluation

D) Student assessment

**Topic: Technology Integration in Physical Education**

**Question 150:** Which technology is often used for assessing physical skills in students?

A) Virtual Reality

B) Heart rate monitors

C) Smartboards

D) Projectors

# Section 5: Collaboration, Reflection, and Technology

**Topic: Professional Development Resources**

**Question 151:** What is the main goal of Continuous Professional Development (CPD) for educators?

A) Salary increase

B) Compliance with state laws

C) Skill and knowledge enhancement

D) Peer recognition

# Section 6: Health Education as a Discipline

## Topic: Introduction to Health Education

**Question 152:** Which organization is responsible for setting health education standards in the U.S.?
A) WHO
B) CDC
C) SHAPE America
D) UNESCO

## Topic: Health Promotion Theories

**Question 153:** Which theory focuses on perceived benefits and barriers to taking action?
A) Social Cognitive Theory
B) Health Belief Model
C) Transtheoretical Model
D) Theory of Reasoned Action

## Topic: Ethics in Health Education

**Question 154:** Which principle requires health educators to respect the autonomy of individuals?
A) Beneficence
B) Non-maleficence
C) Autonomy
D) Justice

## Topic: Community and Public Health

**Question 155:** What is the primary goal of community health education?
A) Disease treatment
B) Disease prevention
C) Rehabilitation
D) Health assessment

# Section 7: Health Education Content

## Topic: Nutrition and Healthy Eating Habits

**Question 156:** Which vitamin is synthesized by exposure to sunlight?
A) Vitamin A
B) Vitamin C
C) Vitamin D
D) Vitamin K

## Topic: Physical Activity and Wellness

**Question 157:** Which exercise primarily focuses on cardiovascular endurance?
A) Weightlifting
B) Running
C) Yoga
D) Stretching

## Topic: Mental and Emotional Health

**Question 158:** What is the key symptom of Generalized Anxiety Disorder (GAD)?

A) Panic attacks

B) Persistent, excessive worry

C) Compulsive behavior

D) Mood swings

## Topic: Substance Abuse Education

**Question 159:** Which substance is classified as a depressant?

A) Cocaine

B) Alcohol

C) Caffeine

D) Nicotine

## Topic: Sexual Health Education

**Question 160:** What is the primary method for preventing sexually transmitted infections (STIs)?

A) Abstinence

B) Vaccination

C) Antibiotics

D) Hormonal birth control

# Section 1: Physical Education Content Knowledge

**Topic: Basics of Physical Education**

**Question 161:** What is the primary objective of adaptive physical education?
A) Competitive sports
B) Specialized training
C) Physical fitness for all
D) Skill development for individuals with disabilities

**Topic: Motor Learning and Skills**

**Question 162:** What is the last stage in Fitts and Posner's stages of motor learning?
A) Cognitive stage
B) Autonomous stage
C) Associative stage
D) Reflexive stage

**Topic: Anatomy and Physiology in Physical Education**

**Question 163:** Which muscle is primarily responsible for elbow flexion?
A) Biceps brachii
B) Triceps brachii
C) Deltoid
D) Latissimus dorsi

**Topic: Sports Psychology**

**Question 164:** What is the term used for the fear of failure in sports psychology?

A) Athlete's burnout

B) Arousal

C) Self-efficacy

D) Performance anxiety

**Topic: Fitness Assessment and Evaluation**

**Question 165:** Which test is commonly used to measure aerobic capacity?

A) VO2 max

B) One-rep max

C) Body Mass Index (BMI)

D) Sit and Reach

# Section 2: Student Growth and Development

**Topic: Childhood Development Theories**

**Question 166:** Who proposed the Zone of Proximal Development theory?

A) Erik Erikson

B) Jean Piaget

C) Lev Vygotsky

D) Sigmund Freud

**Topic: Physical Development Milestones**

**Question 167:** At what age do most children typically start walking?
A) 6-9 months
B) 9-12 months
C) 12-15 months
D) 15-18 months

**Topic: Cognitive Development in Children**

**Question 168:** Which Piagetian stage occurs from approximately 2 to 7 years of age?
A) Sensorimotor
B) Preoperational
C) Concrete Operational
D) Formal Operational

**Topic: Social and Emotional Development**

**Question 169:** Which theorist focused on psychosocial stages of development?
A) Erik Erikson
B) Jean Piaget
C) Lev Vygotsky
D) Sigmund Freud

## Section 3: Management, Motivation, and Communication

**Topic: Classroom Management Techniques**

**Question 170:** Which classroom management approach focuses on democratic decision-making and student choice?
A) Assertive discipline
B) Behavior modification
C) Social contract
D) Classical conditioning

**Topic: Motivational Strategies**

**Question 171:** What is intrinsic motivation?
A) Motivation by external rewards
B) Motivation by fear of punishment
C) Motivation by internal feelings of satisfaction
D) Motivation by peer approval

**Topic: Communication Skills for Teachers**

**Question 172:** Which form of communication involves facial expressions, body language, and gestures?
A) Verbal communication
B) Nonverbal communication
C) Written communication
D) Digital communication

**Topic: Conflict Resolution**

**Question 173:** What is a "win-win" solution in the context of conflict resolution?

A) A solution where one party gains at the expense of another

B) A compromise where both parties give up something

C) A solution where both parties meet their objectives

D) A temporary solution that defers the conflict

## Section 4: Planning, Instruction, and Student Assessment

### Topic: Curriculum Planning and Design

**Question 174:** What is a backward design approach in curriculum planning?

A) Starting with course objectives, then choosing learning activities

B) Starting with learning activities, then defining course objectives

C) Focusing only on formative assessments

D) Focusing only on summative assessments

### Topic: Instructional Strategies

**Question 175:** Which teaching strategy involves students working in pairs or small groups to solve a problem or complete a task?

A) Direct instruction

B) Collaborative learning

C) Independent study

D) Scaffolding

### Topic: Formative and Summative Assessments

**Question 176:** What is the primary purpose of formative assessment?
A) To assign grades
B) To inform future instruction
C) To compare students
D) To certify competence

**Topic: Feedback Mechanisms**

**Question 177:** What type of feedback focuses on the effort and strategies used by the student?
A) Outcome feedback
B) Process feedback
C) Self-comparison feedback
D) Norm-referenced feedback

# Section 5: Collaboration, Reflection, and Technology

**Topic: Teamwork and Collaboration in Education**

**Question 178:** What is the primary goal of a Professional Learning Community (PLC) in education?
A) Networking
B) Faculty management
C) Student achievement
D) Curriculum development

**Topic: Reflective Teaching Practices**

**Question 179:** What type of reflection involves thinking about future actions?

A) Descriptive reflection

B) Dialogic reflection

C) Critical reflection

D) Future action reflection

**Topic: Technology Integration in Physical Education**

**Question 180:** Which technology can be used to monitor students' heart rates during physical activities?

A) Interactive whiteboard

B) Fitness tracker

C) Tablets

D) Virtual Reality headset

**Topic: Professional Development Resources**

**Question 181:** What is a MOOC?

A) An online chat forum for teachers

B) An online course accessible to many

C) A tool for creating digital portfolios

D) A type of educational software

# Section 6: Health Education as a Discipline

**Topic: Introduction to Health Education**

**Question 182:** What is epidemiology?

A) The study of food and nutrition

B) The study of physical exercise

C) The study of diseases and their distribution

D) The study of mental health

**Topic: Health Promotion Theories**

**Question 183:** What does the term "locus of control" refer to in the context of health education?

A) Physical location of health services

B) Individual belief about controlling outcomes

C) Government regulations on health

D) Community resources for health

**Topic: Ethics in Health Education**

**Question 184:** What principle in ethics in health education focuses on doing good for the community or individual?

A) Autonomy

B) Justice

C) Beneficence

D) Non-maleficence

**Topic: Community and Public Health**

**Question 185:** What is a "health disparity"?

A) Uniformity in health outcomes

B) An infectious disease

C) Inequality in health across different populations

D) Effective healthcare system

## Section 7: Health Education Content

### Topic: Nutrition and Healthy Eating Habits

**Question 186:** What is the role of fiber in the diet?

A) To provide energy

B) To aid in digestion

C) To build muscle

D) To store fat

### Topic: Physical Activity and Wellness

**Question 187:** What is anaerobic exercise?

A) Exercise that requires oxygen

B) Exercise that does not require oxygen

C) Low-intensity exercise

D) Prolonged exercise

### Topic: Mental and Emotional Health

**Question 188:** What is mindfulness?

A) Focusing on the past

B) Focusing on the future

C) Focusing on the present moment
D) Ignoring the surroundings

**Topic: Substance Abuse Education**

**Question 189:** What substance is primarily responsible for the effects of tobacco?
A) THC
B) Caffeine
C) Nicotine
D) Alcohol

**Topic: Sexual Health Education**

**Question 190:** What is the primary purpose of a contraceptive?
A) To treat sexually transmitted infections
B) To enhance sexual performance
C) To prevent pregnancy
D) To regulate hormones

# Section 1: Physical Education Content Knowledge

**Topic: Basics of Physical Education**

**Question 191:** What is the primary goal of physical education?
A) Athletic development
B) Academic achievement

C) Physical fitness
D) Social interaction

## Section 2: Student Growth and Development

### Topic: Childhood Development Theories

**Question 192:** Who developed the theory of cognitive development?
A) Erik Erikson
B) Jean Piaget
C) Abraham Maslow
D) B.F. Skinner

## Section 3: Management, Motivation, and Communication

### Topic: Classroom Management Techniques

**Question 193:** What technique involves providing clear instructions and cues to manage classroom behavior?
A) Positive reinforcement
B) Modeling
C) Direct instruction
D) Punishment

## Section 4: Planning, Instruction, and Student Assessment

**Topic: Curriculum Planning and Design**

**Question 194:** What is the first step in developing a curriculum?

A) Selecting learning materials

B) Establishing learning objectives

C) Defining evaluation metrics

D) Deciding teaching methods

## Section 5: Collaboration, Reflection, and Technology

**Topic: Reflective Teaching Practices**

**Question 195:** What reflective practice involves teachers observing their own teaching methods?

A) Peer review

B) Self-assessment

C) Journal writing

D) Student feedback

## Section 6: Health Education as a Discipline

**Topic: Community and Public Health**

**Question 196:** What is a pandemic?

A) A localized disease outbreak

B) A global disease outbreak

C) A recurring seasonal illness

D) A mild disease affecting a community

# Section 7: Health Education Content

## Topic: Substance Abuse Education

**Question 197:** What is the psychoactive component in cannabis?
A) CBD
B) THC
C) Nicotine
D) Caffeine

# Section 1: Physical Education Content Knowledge

## Topic: Motor Learning and Skills

**Question 198:** Which stage of motor learning is characterized by inconsistent performance?
A) Autonomous stage
B) Cognitive stage
C) Associative stage
D) Refinement stage

# Section 2: Student Growth and Development

## Topic: Cognitive Development in Children

**Question 199:** What is object permanence?

A) The understanding that shapes remain constant

B) The understanding that objects continue to exist when out of sight

C) The ability to perceive depth

D) The ability to categorize objects

## Section 5: Collaboration, Reflection, and Technology

### Topic: Technology Integration in Physical Education

**Question 200:** What is a common use for augmented reality in physical education?

A) Virtual field trips

B) Live streaming classes

C) Skill demonstration

D) Gamified activities

# 9.2 ANSWER SHEET – PRACTICE TEST 2

**101. Answer:** C) Physical fitness
**Explanation:** The primary objective of physical education is to promote physical fitness among students.

**102. Answer:** B) Skills performed in a predictable environment
**Explanation:** Closed skills are performed in a predictable, stable environment where the performer controls the performance situation.

**103. Answer:** B) Smooth
**Explanation:** Smooth muscles control involuntary actions like the movement of the digestive system.

**104. Answer:** B) Operant Conditioning
**Explanation:** Operant Conditioning focuses on the role of reinforcement and punishment in shaping behavior, including motivation.

**105. Answer:** A) 1.5-mile run
**Explanation:** The 1.5-mile run is a commonly used field test for assessing cardiovascular fitness.

**106. Answer:** D) Piaget
**Explanation:** Jean Piaget proposed the theory of cognitive development, which includes the sensorimotor and preoperational stages among others.

**107. Answer:** C) 12-15 months

**Explanation:** Most children typically begin to walk between 12 and 15 months.

**108. Answer:** C) Concrete Operational

**Explanation:** In Piaget's theory, children in the Concrete Operational stage begin to think logically about concrete events.

**109. Answer:** B) Ability to manage emotions

**Explanation:** Emotional regulation refers to the ability to manage and respond to emotional experiences in a socially acceptable manner.

**110. Answer:** B) Students earn tokens for good behavior

**Explanation:** In a token economy system, students earn tokens for good behavior, which can be exchanged for rewards.

**111. Answer:** B) Motivation from internal rewards

**Explanation:** Intrinsic motivation comes from internal rewards like personal satisfaction or enjoyment.

**112. Answer:** C) Listening with full attention and providing feedback

**Explanation:** Active listening involves giving full attention to the speaker and providing feedback to show that you understand.

**113. Answer:** D) Collaborating

**Explanation:** The collaborative style of conflict resolution seeks win-win solutions where all parties' needs are met.

**114. Answer:** B) A curriculum that revisits topics at increasing levels of difficulty

**Explanation:** A spiral curriculum revisits topics at different grade levels, each time at increasing levels of difficulty.

**115. Answer:** C) Question and answer dialogue

**Explanation:** The Socratic method involves a form of cooperative argumentative dialogue to stimulate critical thinking.

**116. Answer:** B) Quiz

**Explanation:** Quizzes are formative assessments that provide feedback during the instructional process.

**117. Answer:** C) Feedback that helps improve performance

**Explanation:** Constructive feedback is designed to provide specific, actionable information to help improve performance.

**118. Answer:** C) Learning in small groups

**Explanation:** Collaborative learning involves learning in small groups where students work together to solve a problem or complete a task.

**119. Answer:** B) To showcase a teacher's best practices

**Explanation:** A teaching portfolio is used to showcase a teacher's best practices, achievements, and competencies in teaching.

**120. Answer:** B) Biometric sensors

**Explanation:** Biometric sensors can provide real-time analysis of a student's running form, including gait analysis and biomechanical feedback.

**121. Answer:** C) To improve teaching skills and strategies

**Explanation:** The primary purpose of attending professional development workshops is to improve teaching skills and strategies.

**122. Answer:** D) All of the above

**Explanation:** Health education focuses on physical fitness, disease prevention, and emotional well-being, aiming for a holistic approach to health.

**123. Answer:** B) The role of individual beliefs in health behavior

**Explanation:** The Health Belief Model focuses on the role of individual beliefs in determining health behavior.

**124. Answer:** C) Understanding and agreeing to participate

**Explanation:** Informed consent in health education means that the individual understands what they will be participating in and agrees to it.

**125. Answer:** B) Study of diseases and how they spread

**Explanation:** Epidemiology is the study of how diseases spread and can be controlled within populations.

**126. Answer:** C) Number of calories per gram of food

**Explanation:** Caloric density refers to the number of calories contained per gram of food.

**127. Answer:** B) 150 minutes

**Explanation:** The general guideline for adults is at least 150 minutes of moderate exercise per week.

**128. Answer:** B) Awareness of present moment

**Explanation:** Mindfulness is the awareness and acceptance of the present moment.

**129. Answer:** C) To prevent misuse

**Explanation:** The primary purpose of substance abuse education is to prevent the misuse of substances.

**130. Answer:** A) Abstinence

**Explanation:** Abstinence from sexual activity is the most effective method for preventing STIs.

**131. Answer:** D) Skill development

**Explanation:** The primary goal of physical education is the development of motor skills, physical fitness, and the cognitive and emotional aspects related to physical activities.

**132. Answer:** B) Awareness of body position

**Explanation:** Kinesthetic awareness refers to the awareness of the position and movement of the body.

**133. Answer:** C) Cardiac muscle

**Explanation:** The heart is mainly composed of cardiac muscle.

**134. Answer:** B) Peak performance state

**Explanation:** "Flow state" refers to a state of peak performance where an individual is fully immersed in the activity.

**135. Answer:** C) Aerobic capacity

**Explanation:** VO2 max measures the maximum rate of oxygen consumption during incremental exercise.

**136. Answer:** C) Erikson

**Explanation:** Erik Erikson proposed the theory of psychosocial development, which outlines the social tasks an individual must accomplish at various ages.

**137. Answer:** B) 10-14 months

**Explanation:** Most children start walking between 10-14 months of age.

**138. Answer:** B) Understanding that objects exist even when not seen

**Explanation:** Object permanence is the cognitive understanding that objects continue to exist even when they cannot be seen.

**139. Answer:** C) Understanding and sharing another person's feelings

**Explanation:** Empathy is the ability to understand and share the feelings of another.

**140. Answer:** B) To facilitate learning

**Explanation:** The main goal of a classroom management plan is to create an environment conducive to learning.

**141. Answer:** B) Trophy

**Explanation:** Extrinsic motivation is driven by external rewards like trophies, money, or grades.

**142. Answer:** B) Linear model

**Explanation:** In the linear model of communication, a sender encodes a message and sends it to a receiver who decodes it.

**143. Answer:** A) Issue

**Explanation:** "I-Messages" usually start with the word "I" and focus on the issue, allowing the sender to take responsibility for their feelings and thoughts.

**144. Answer:** D) Community-Centered

**Explanation:** Common types of curriculum design include Subject-Centered, Learner-Centered, and Problem-Centered. Community-Centered is not a standard type.

**145. Answer:** B) Support mechanism to aid learning

**Explanation:** Scaffolding is a teaching method that involves providing initial support that is gradually removed as the learner becomes more competent.

**146. Answer:** A) Formative

**Explanation:** Formative assessment is conducted during the learning process to provide ongoing feedback.

**147. Answer:** C) Task-specific feedback

**Explanation:** Task-specific feedback focuses on the task and how it can be improved, rather than focusing on the learner's abilities.

**148. Answer:** B) Group of educators committed to working collaboratively

**Explanation:** A Professional Learning Community (PLC) is a group of educators who meet regularly to share expertise and collaborate on instructional practices.

**149. Answer:** B) Self-assessment and improvement

**Explanation:** The primary purpose of reflective teaching is for teachers to assess and improve their own teaching practices.

**150. Answer:** B) Heart rate monitors

**Explanation:** Heart rate monitors are commonly used in physical education for assessing physical exertion and cardiovascular fitness.

**151. Answer:** C) Skill and knowledge enhancement

**Explanation:** The main goal of Continuous Professional Development (CPD) is to improve educators' skills and knowledge, thereby enhancing their teaching effectiveness.

**152. Answer:** C) SHAPE America

**Explanation:** SHAPE America (Society of Health and Physical Educators) sets the standards for health education in the United States.

**153. Answer:** B) Health Belief Model

**Explanation:** The Health Belief Model focuses on the perceptions of the risks and benefits, as well as barriers to taking action.

**154. Answer:** C) Autonomy

**Explanation:** The principle of autonomy emphasizes the importance of respecting an individual's capacity for self-determination.

**155. Answer:** B) Disease prevention

**Explanation:** The primary goal of community health education is to prevent disease and promote health in the community.

**156. Answer:** C) Vitamin D

**Explanation:** Vitamin D is synthesized when the skin is exposed to sunlight.

**157. Answer:** B) Running

**Explanation:** Running is an aerobic exercise that primarily focuses on cardiovascular endurance.

**158. Answer:** B) Persistent, excessive worry

**Explanation:** Generalized Anxiety Disorder (GAD) is characterized by persistent, excessive worry about various aspects of life.

**159. Answer:** B) Alcohol

**Explanation:** Alcohol is a depressant, meaning it slows down the central nervous system.

**160. Answer:** A) Abstinence

**Explanation:** Abstinence from sexual activity is the most effective method for preventing STIs.

**161. Answer:** D) Skill development for individuals with disabilities

**Explanation:** Adaptive physical education is designed to meet the unique needs of individuals with disabilities, focusing on skill development tailored for them.

**162. Answer:** B) Autonomous stage

**Explanation:** The Autonomous stage is the final stage in Fitts and Posner's model of motor learning, where the movement becomes automatic.

**163. Answer:** A) Biceps brachii

**Explanation:** The biceps brachii is the primary muscle responsible for elbow flexion.

**164. Answer:** D) Performance anxiety

**Explanation:** The fear of failure in sports psychology is often referred to as performance anxiety.

**165. Answer:** A) VO2 max

**Explanation:** VO2 max is commonly used to measure aerobic capacity.

**166. Answer:** C) Lev Vygotsky

**Explanation:** Lev Vygotsky proposed the Zone of Proximal Development theory, which focuses on the difference between what a learner can do without help and what they can do with help.

**167. Answer:** C) 12-15 months

**Explanation:** Most children start walking between the ages of 12-15 months.

**168. Answer:** B) Preoperational

**Explanation:** According to Jean Piaget, the Preoperational stage occurs from approximately 2 to 7 years of age.

**169. Answer:** A) Erik Erikson

**Explanation:** Erik Erikson is known for his theory of psychosocial stages of development, which emphasizes the impact of social experience across the lifespan.

**170. Answer:** C) Social contract

**Explanation:** The social contract approach to classroom management focuses on democratic decision-making and allows for student choice and shared responsibilities.

**171. Answer:** C) Motivation by internal feelings of satisfaction

**Explanation:** Intrinsic motivation is driven by internal feelings of satisfaction and personal reward, rather than external factors.

**172. Answer:** B) Nonverbal communication

**Explanation:** Nonverbal communication involves facial expressions, body language, and gestures, and it can provide additional context to verbal messages.

**173. Answer:** C) A solution where both parties meet their objectives

**Explanation:** A "win-win" solution in conflict resolution is one where both parties meet their objectives, ensuring mutual satisfaction.

**174. Answer:** A) Starting with course objectives, then choosing learning activities

**Explanation:** In a backward design approach, curriculum planning starts by defining the desired learning outcomes or objectives, followed by selecting appropriate learning activities and assessments.

**175. Answer:** B) Collaborative learning

**Explanation:** Collaborative learning involves students working together in pairs or small groups to solve a problem or complete a task.

**176. Answer:** B) To inform future instruction

**Explanation:** The primary purpose of formative assessment is to gather data that informs future instruction and supports ongoing learning.

**177. Answer:** B) Process feedback

**Explanation:** Process feedback focuses on the effort and strategies used by the student, encouraging them to understand the learning process.

**178. Answer:** C) Student achievement

**Explanation:** The primary goal of a Professional Learning Community (PLC) is to improve student achievement through collaborative efforts among educators.

**179. Answer:** D) Future action reflection

**Explanation:** Future action reflection involves thinking about how you will act in similar situations in the future based on your reflection.

**180. Answer:** B) Fitness tracker

**Explanation:** Fitness trackers can monitor students' heart rates during physical activities, providing valuable data for both students and teachers.

**181. Answer:** B) An online course accessible to many

**Explanation:** MOOC stands for Massive Open Online Course, which is an online course accessible to many people and often free of charge.

**182. Answer:** C) The study of diseases and their distribution

**Explanation:** Epidemiology is the study of how diseases affect the health and illness of populations.

**183. Answer:** B) Individual belief about controlling outcomes

**Explanation:** In the context of health education, "locus of control" refers to an individual's belief about how much they can control their own health outcomes.

**184. Answer:** C) Beneficence

**Explanation:** The principle of beneficence focuses on doing good either for the individual or the community as a whole.

**185. Answer:** C) Inequality in health across different populations

**Explanation:** A health disparity refers to a higher burden of illness, injury, disability, or mortality experienced by one population group relative to another group.

**186. Answer:** B) To aid in digestion

**Explanation:** Fiber aids in digestion by helping to move food through the digestive system and promoting regular bowel movements.

**187. Answer:** B) Exercise that does not require oxygen

**Explanation:** Anaerobic exercise is a high-intensity, short-duration activity that does not require oxygen for fuel.

**188. Answer:** C) Focusing on the present moment

**Explanation:** Mindfulness involves focusing on the present moment, often as a way to improve mental and emotional well-being.

**189. Answer:** C) Nicotine

**Explanation:** Nicotine is the substance primarily responsible for the addictive effects of tobacco.

**190. Answer:** C) To prevent pregnancy

**Explanation:** The primary purpose of a contraceptive is to prevent pregnancy.

**191. Answer:** C) Physical fitness

**Explanation:** The primary goal of physical education is to develop physical fitness and to educate students on the importance of activity.

**192. Answer:** B) Jean Piaget

**Explanation:** Jean Piaget developed the theory of cognitive development, which explores how children understand the world around them.

**193. Answer:** C) Direct instruction

**Explanation:** Direct instruction involves providing clear, concise instructions and cues to help manage classroom behavior effectively.

**194. Answer:** B) Establishing learning objectives

**Explanation:** The first step in developing a curriculum is establishing clear learning objectives to guide the teaching and evaluation process.

**195. Answer:** B) Self-assessment

**Explanation:** Self-assessment involves teachers observing and evaluating their own teaching methods to improve practice.

**196. Answer:** B) A global disease outbreak

**Explanation:** A pandemic is a global outbreak of a disease affecting people over multiple countries or continents.

**197. Answer:** B) THC

**Explanation:** THC (tetrahydrocannabinol) is the psychoactive component in cannabis responsible for the 'high'.

**198. Answer:** B) Cognitive stage

**Explanation:** The cognitive stage of motor learning is characterized by inconsistent performance and frequent errors.

**199. Answer:** B) The understanding that objects continue to exist when out of sight

**Explanation:** Object permanence is the cognitive understanding that objects continue to exist even when they are not visible.

**200. Answer:** D) Gamified activities

**Explanation:** Augmented reality is commonly used to create gamified activities that make physical education more engaging for students.

# TEST-TAKING STRATEGIES

As you prepare for the Praxis Health and Physical Education Content Knowledge 5857 exam, it's not just what you know but also how you apply your knowledge that can make all the difference. This section provides essential test-taking strategies and tips to help you excel on exam day while also addressing the common challenge of test anxiety.

## Test-Taking Strategies:

1. **Read the Questions Carefully:** Begin by reading each question carefully. Pay close attention to keywords like "not," "except," or "best." Misreading a question can lead to incorrect answers.

2. **Manage Your Time:** The Praxis exam is timed, so allocate your time wisely. Answer questions you're confident about first, and come back to more challenging ones later.

3. **Eliminate Obvious Wrong Answers:** If you're uncertain about an answer, eliminate choices that are clearly incorrect. This increases your chances of selecting the right one.

4. **Use Process of Elimination:** When unsure, narrow down your choices by eliminating the least likely answers. This can help you make an educated guess.

5. **Don't Second-Guess Too Much:** While it's essential to review your answers, avoid changing them unless you're sure of the correction. Your initial instinct is often correct.

6. **Answer All Questions:** In the Praxis exam, there is no penalty for guessing. If you're running out of time, make educated guesses on unanswered questions.

7. **Stay Calm:** If you encounter a difficult question, take a deep breath and stay calm. Stress can impair your ability to think clearly.

## Overcoming Test Anxiety:

Test anxiety is a common challenge, but there are strategies to manage it:

1. **Practice Under Exam Conditions:** Simulate exam conditions during your practice tests to become more comfortable with the experience.

2. **Relaxation Techniques:** Learn relaxation techniques, such as deep breathing and meditation, to calm your nerves.

3. **Healthy Lifestyle:** Maintain a healthy lifestyle with regular exercise, a balanced diet, and adequate sleep to help manage stress.

4. **Positive Visualization:** Visualize your success. Imagine yourself confidently answering questions during the exam.

5. **Focus on the Present:** Concentrate on one question at a time. Don't dwell on previous questions or worry about what's ahead.

6. **Arrive Early:** On exam day, arrive early to reduce stress from rushing or being late.

7. **Use Positive Affirmations:** Replace negative thoughts with positive affirmations about your abilities.

**Takeaway:**

Remember, preparation and confidence are your allies. This study guide is your trusted companion on your journey to success. Utilize these test-taking strategies to answer questions effectively, and employ techniques to manage test anxiety.

Your dedication and hard work will pay off, and you'll be well-prepared to tackle the Praxis Health and Physical Education Content Knowledge 5857 exam. Test Treasure Publication is here to support you every step of the way, from exam preparation to your fulfilling career as a health and physical education teacher.

# ADDITIONAL RESOURCES

To excel in the Praxis Health and Physical Education Content Knowledge 5857 exam, it's essential to have access to a variety of resources that can enhance your understanding of the subjects and provide additional support. This section presents a selection of recommended online resources and academic materials to complement your study.

## Recommended Online Resources:

1. **Educational Testing Service (ETS):** The official Praxis website by ETS offers valuable resources, including test preparation materials, practice tests, and exam information. (Website: www.ets.org/praxis)

2. **Praxis Study Guides:** ETS provides official study guides for each Praxis exam, including practice questions and test-taking tips. These are excellent resources for exam preparation.

3. **Khan Academy:** Khan Academy offers free video lessons and practice questions in various subjects, including health and physical education. (Website: www.khanacademy.org)

4. **Quizlet:** Quizlet is a platform where you can find flashcards and study materials created by educators and students. It's an excellent resource for self-assessment and review. (Website: www.quizlet.com)

5. **Study.com:** Study.com offers courses and study guides on health and physical education topics, providing in-depth explanations and practice questions. (Website: www.study.com)

6. **YouTube:** YouTube hosts a wealth of educational channels covering health and physical education topics. You can find video lessons, tutorials, and explanations on various subjects.

## Recommended Academic Materials:

1. **"Physical Education Methods for Elementary Teachers" by Jerry Thomas and Lynn Housner:** This book is a valuable guide for understanding physical education methods and instructional strategies.

2. **"Praxis Health and Physical Education Content Knowledge for Educators" by Philip LeConte:** This book provides a comprehensive overview of the topics covered in the exam, with practice questions and answers.

3. **"Health and Physical Education for Elementary Classroom Teachers" by Retta Evans and Sandra Hagen Hopkins:** This book covers the fundamental concepts of health and physical education, providing insights into teaching strategies and content knowledge.

4. **"Essentials of Strength Training and Conditioning" by Thomas R. Baechle and Roger W. Earle:** For those studying physical education, this book offers insights into strength training and conditioning, which may be covered in the exam.

5. **"Health Education: Elementary and Middle School Applications" by Susan Telljohann, Cynthia Symons, and Beverly P. Wood:** This academic resource focuses on health education in elementary and mid-

dle school settings.

These recommended online resources and academic materials can complement your study with diverse perspectives, practice questions, and in-depth knowledge. Utilize them to strengthen your understanding and preparation for the Praxis exam.

# FINAL WORDS

As you reach the end of this study guide, you've completed a significant step on your journey to becoming a certified health and physical education teacher. You've acquired knowledge, honed your skills, and prepared yourself for the challenges and opportunities that lie ahead.

We understand that the path you've chosen is not without its hurdles, but remember this: Every step you take brings you closer to your goal. Teaching health and physical education is more than a profession; it's a calling to shape the future, to inspire young minds, and to instill a lifelong love for well-being and physical activity.

The Praxis Health and Physical Education Content Knowledge 5857 exam is your gateway to this rewarding career. As you prepare for it, keep these words in your heart:

**1. You Are Capable:** You possess the intelligence, dedication, and passion needed to excel in this field. Trust in your abilities and knowledge.

**2. Challenges Are Opportunities:** Challenges are not roadblocks but stepping stones. Each obstacle you overcome makes you stronger and wiser.

**3. Persistence Pays Off:** The journey may be tough, but your perseverance will lead to success. Keep going, even when it's challenging.

**4. Make a Difference:** The knowledge you gain is not just for your benefit; it's a gift you'll share with countless students. Your guidance can transform lives.

**5. Embrace Lifelong Learning:** Teaching is a lifelong journey of growth and adaptation. Stay curious, continue learning, and evolve with the times.

**6. Support Is All Around:** You are not alone on this path. Seek guidance from mentors, connect with fellow educators, and utilize the resources available to you.

**7. Your Success Inspires Others:** Your success will inspire others to pursue their dreams. Be a beacon of hope and a source of motivation for those who follow in your footsteps.

**8. Keep the Passion Alive:** Remember why you chose this path. Your passion for health and physical education can light up a classroom and ignite the same passion in your students.

In closing, we want you to know that Test Treasure Publication is here to support you at every stage of your educational and professional journey. We believe in your potential and are committed to helping you achieve your goals.

With your dedication, the knowledge you've gained from this study guide, and the belief in your abilities, you're well on your way to making a lasting impact as a health and physical education teacher. The future is bright, and you're an essential part of it.

Go forth with confidence, purpose, and a heart filled with the desire to make a positive difference in the lives of your students. Your adventure begins now, and it holds the promise of extraordinary success.

Best wishes on your path to becoming a certified health and physical education teacher!

# EXPLORE OUR RANGE OF STUDY GUIDES

At Test Treasure Publication, we understand that academic success requires more than just raw intelligence or tireless effort—it requires targeted preparation. That's why we offer an extensive range of study guides, meticulously designed to help you excel in various exams across the USA.

## Our Offerings

- **Medical Exams:** Conquer the MCAT, USMLE, and more with our comprehensive study guides, complete with practice questions and diagnostic tests.

- **Law Exams:** Get a leg up on the LSAT and bar exams with our tailored resources, offering theoretical insights and practical exercises.

- **Business and Management Tests:** Ace the GMAT and other business exams with our incisive guides, equipped with real-world examples and scenarios.

- **Engineering & Technical Exams:** Prep for the FE, PE, and other technical exams with our specialized guides, which delve into both fundamentals and complexities.

- **High School Exams:** Be it the SAT, ACT, or AP tests, our high school range is designed to give you a competitive edge.

- **State-Specific Exams:** Tailored resources to help you with exams unique to specific states, whether it's teacher qualification exams or state civil service exams.

## Why Choose Test Treasure Publication?

- **Comprehensive Coverage:** Each guide covers all essential topics in detail.

- **Quality Material:** Crafted by experts in each field.

- **Interactive Tools:** Flashcards, online quizzes, and downloadable resources to complement your study.

- **Customizable Learning:** Personalize your prep journey by focusing on areas where you need the most help.

- **Community Support:** Access to online forums where you can discuss concerns, seek guidance, and share success stories.

## Contact Us

For inquiries about our study guides, or to provide feedback, please email us at support@testtreasure.com.

## Order Now

Ready to elevate your preparation to the next level? Visit our website www.testtreasure.com to browse our complete range of study guides and make your purchase.

Made in the USA
Middletown, DE
27 February 2025